Mirror of Doubt

Can You Solve the JFK Conspiracy?

by

Robin T. DeLoria

DORRANCE PUBLISHING CO., INC.
PITTSBURGH, PENNSYLVANIA 15222

Special Dedication

Dedicated to the men from Newcomb, New York who served in the armed forces in Vietnam.

Robert Dubay	Leo Kushi	David Shaughnessy
Bruce Friend	Charles Luce	Wayne Smith
Michael Garrand	Wayne Moorehouse	Chris Sorensen
Terry Garrand	David Moses	Jens Sorensen
Paige Garvey, Jr.	Michael Moses	Hayden Stickney
John Hall	Mitchell Moses	Kenneth Stickney
Joe Helms	Floyd Buzzy Norton	Robert Stringer
Robert Helms	Harry Parker	Daniel Tefoe, Jr.
Richard Hunter	Hugh Pasco, Jr.	Forrest Tierson
	James Porter	

With courage, honor, and dignity, these men served. All returned safely.

Also to my parents, friends, loved ones, and family. Your support, encouragement, concern, guidance, and interest in this work truly made reaching the end of the path possible. To you I will always be grateful.

Thanks to Apple Computer, U-Compute, Plattsburgh, New York; The Lane Press, Burlington, Vermont; Jamie Silverberg and Robert Groden; and Jonathan Myers of the Assassination and Research Center, Washington, D.C.

Contents

Introduction

Mirror of Doubt: Can You Solve the JFK Conspiracy? is based on evidence of the Kennedy Assassination that never reached the American public. The intent of the book is to focus on facts and evidence that would have shed different light on Dealey Plaza in 1963 when President John F. Kennedy was assassinated. It will, by analysis of photographic and physical evidence, examine eyewitness testimony and raise questions concerning the contradiction of the facts. This will not be a long, drawn-out book on the assassination, but will be formatted in laymen's terms, so that each of us will have an opportunity to understand. It is intended to focus on that dreadful day in Dallas twenty-eight years ago, to inspire truth, and to wipe away the reasonable doubt that each of us has carried sinse that day.

If you were too young to remember the assassination, as I was, this will be a history lesson. If you remember, but feel deep down inside that the truth is yet to be told, you will find the truth here. *Mirror of Doubt* is an information guide that you can use to view the relevant facts pertaining to the assassination, as if you were standing in Dealey Plaza on 22 November 1963 when President Kennedy was shot. *Mirror of Doubt* will relax your suspicions and validate your sense of reasoning and understanding. The truth will be easy as you witness the grand illusion that took the life of this nation's president, leaving you helpless to ever knowing the truth about that day. This book will also discuss Lee Harvey Oswald, who was determined to be the lone assassin, but it will not be his biography. The Warren Commission did a fine job with that, so well leave that topic alone. If the evidence is confusing, then so must the truth be! The truth must be attested to by those who took part in the assassination.

The many eyewitnesses, members of the motorcade, along with the many photographs taken on that day have still failed to produce a vivid depiction of the actual events. The assassination of President Kennedy has left acquisitive results and the Warren Commission's report failed to satisfy our intellectual need to hear the truth. People in general are intelligent and the Warren Commission did not give us all the facts about the event.

If it had, you would know who shot John F. Kennedy today. As we will learn, the Commission knew but would not disclose this information.

The evidence you will examine in *Mirror of Doubt* casts a veil of suspicion upon the Warren Commission members and the Federal Bureau of Investigation. If they knew a conspiracy had taken place, why didn't they tell us? A conspiracy did take place and *Mirror of Doubt* will reveal it to you. We will go back thirty years to a paradox of unanswered questions harbored in the annex of time as we address even the most complicated aspects of the assassination. You will understand how the president's death became a mystery, who covered it up, and why it was coverered up for all these years. We will examine evidence of two conspiracies: One by the murderers of the president and the other by our own government in a plot designed to keep the circumstances surrounding the president's death and the shooting of John Connally a secret.

Mirror of Doubt is not a theory.

The evidence that has always compounded my belief that a conspiracy did take place has also left me with sheer astonishment of those who have precluded certain facts in their attempts to get at the truth. Many authors and historians have pointed fingers into theories that have been discounted; yet theories are but mere supposition, a way for people to say, "I see it like this," or "It happened this way." But if we can't see it, then we can't believe it. The trouble with stating a theory is that it's only a theory and must be proven beyond a reasonable doubt. We cannot say that it never happened, nor can we confuse the issue by stating things which can never be proven. The facts that tell a different story, have not reached the American public.

I was five years old when President Kennedy was assassinated, but I have sinse joined the many hundreds of individuals who have sought after the truth that transpired on that day in Dallas. I have never been satisfied with the conclusions documented by the Warren Commission and have always known deep down inside that someday the truth would be known.

Over the years I have collected much information concerning the assassination. The information that I initially used to look into the event dates back to the late sixties. Four years had passed sinse the Commission had handed over its decision and the public sector expressed concern that the Warren Report had overlooked crucial evidence. Once-disputed evidence by the Commission was now bringing heartfelt cries from concerned individuals who simply wouldn't accept the lone gunman ruling. The Abraham Zapruder film showed *beyond a reasonable doubt* that the third and fatal shot that killed the President came from the front, not from behind as the Report stated. The Commission was wrong! Evidence of a second gunman in Dealey Plaza was substantiated in the form of hard evidence on eight millimeter film recorded by Abraham Zapruder. Was the Commission intentionally wrong?

The Warren Report, in my opinion, is a cleverly devised tale constructed to hide the truth about what happened in Dallas. I believe, too, that not all the members of the Commission concluded that Lee Harvey Oswald was the sole assassin; nor do I defend the incompleteness of the Commission's official report. The Warren Commission was a by-product of our democratic government and it was its job to research the assassination and find the truth. It did a lousy job of reporting the facts and bringing the truth to the sight of the American people. The evidence against Lee Harvey Oswald was at best circumstantial, but that is not what the members of the Commission wanted us to believe.

If the Warren Commission had all the facts relevant to making a decision as to what happened, then I believe that everyone would have been satisfied with its report. The question is, do we have all the facts? The Commission consisted of eight members. It had an assistant council with a staff totaling more than twenty-six. The Commission's resources, the United States government, was the largest, single, political entity in the entire world at the time. The simple conclusion reached by the Commission after nearly a year of concentrated efforts by law enforcement professionals and attorneys was that Lee Harvey Oswald acted alone, firing three shots from the Texas School Book Depository. One bullet struck the president and Governor Connally, another missed both men, and the third struck only the president resulting in his death. This conclusion caused widespread controversy and the fact remained that Lee Harvey Oswald shot no one. He was framed by conspirators and our government, but had no part in the assassination. We'll find Oswald innocent, but was there another gunman on the sixth floor of the Book Depository? How many shots were fired? How many gunmen were present in Dealey Plaza? Did one bullet cause all the wounds sustained by the president and Governor Connally?

The Commission concluded that either the first or second bullet hit both men. There were only three shots fired and the third hit just the president. Even though the Commission could not substantiate the involvement of others (as we will learn it suggested), it nevertheless concluded that all the shots were fired from above and behind the presidential motorcade and that there was no credible evidence to suggest that the shots were fired from anywhere else. Was there evidence to indicate that the bullets were fired from the front or from a location other than the Depository? If so, what became of this evidence and why wasn't it filed in the Official Report?

Diagram 1

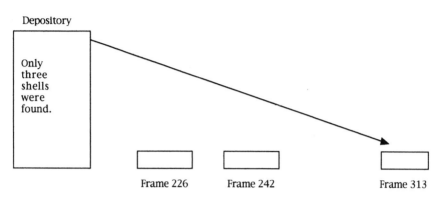

Frame 313–Kennedy is struck by this bullet. His head is propelled violently backwards by the impact of this shot. This is a clear indication of a conspiracy as one of the three cartridges would have had to have been planted.

Even the Zapruder film failed to reach the suspicions of the Commission and its staff. The third shot alone was credible evidence that at least one gunman fired from the front. It hit only the president and established the presence of another gunman in Dealey Plaza. There were two gunmen in Dealey Plaza; neither of which, in my opinion and based on the facts in this case, could have been located on the sixth floor of the Depository. By looking into *Mirror of Doubt* you will learn the Warren Commission would not accept what it could not prove. The irony? It knew!

If you never had the chance to see the Zapruder film, you are not alone. Many millions of people have never seen it. In the final sequence of the film as the third bullet makes contact with the president, his head is propelled violently backwards. If he was hit from behind, we could expect the opposite reaction of this, whereby the president would have slumped immediately forward from the impact of the bullet. Instead the president's head responded in a violent backwards motion and he collapsed into the car seat. As you will learn, the Commission went into great detail to prove the impossible and convince the American public of Lee Harvey Oswald's guilt. The motion of the president's head was deemed by the Commission as a reaction caused when the bullet exited the front of his head. This is not possible! The head being propelled backwards was a clear result of a bullet entering his head from the front and the trajectory of this bullet, regardless of direction, was clearly established by medical findings. Front or rear entry, according to history, has yet to be determined.

JFK—the Movie

Oliver Stone, the Hollywood film director, created a monumental film that many will enjoy and come to admire. His talents have produced a paradox in history, a way for people to return to Dealey Plaza on that dreadful day in 1963 when President John F. Kennedy was assassinated. Mr. Stone, as have many others, has succeeded in weakening the stability of the Warren Report, bringing to life evidence discounted for reasons of doubt. The film is history, but not in regard to the events recorded by the Warren Commission. What really happened in Dallas though, Mr. Stone does not address in the movie *JFK*.

Perhaps the visions of New Orleans District Attorney Jim Garrison and the others of his staff fostered the belief that Oliver Stone so uniquely represents, that a cover-up may not have been linked to members of the Commission if the information never got there to begin with. But did the Warren Commission know that a cover-up was taking place? Were there facts to substantiate the presence of a lone gunman, other than Lee Harvey Oswald, firing at the president? Who then, the FBI, the CIA, the White House? Someone knew something and no one was talking. The facts and testimony collected were conclusive, but the government simply didn't want you to know.

Jim Garrison, on the other hand, wasn't about to let his country go down the tubes without a fight. In my opinion Garrison should be recognized as a mastermind in his own right. He knew that Clay Shaw may have had ties to Lee Harvey Oswald and David Ferrie, but what Garrison needed was a patsy, a Lee Harvey Oswald of his own. He knew that in his effort to shed light on the truth that his life would be in danger. Think of it. If Garrison could be labeled as a fool by the conspirators, they would be safe with the notion of Garrison charging Shaw with the conspiracy. Yet Garrison would have an opportunity to shed light on the assassination, which was the result of a high-level government conspiracy and a subsequent cover-up by the Warren Commission and the FBI.

The Truth

All the facts concerning the assassination have not been released to the public. Some are contained within the twenty-six volumes of the Warren Report, but the condensed, hardcover version printed and distributed to the general public can best be described as an oversight report and does not contain the facts relevant to disclosing the truth. In my opinion the Warren Report is the unauthorized biography of Lee Harvey Oswald. Of this eight-hundred-page report, two hundred pages are devoted to the president's death and the other six hundred to Lee Harvey Oswald's supposed involvement. Lee Harvey Oswald was a patsy and the facts about Dallas 1963 suggest an entirely different event occurring. The purpose of freeing your mind from Oswald firing the shots in Dallas is that you have been brainwashed into believing just that. The facts will convince you otherwise and it is my intent to give you a head start.

A noted philosopher once said, "Truth is quite beyond the reach of satire. There is so brave a simplicity in it, that it can no more be made ridiculous that an oak or a pine."

The word *truth* reminds me of a true story told by a very close and dear friend. It was told to me during the early part of my research and I will admit that I did share with him the information I am writing here today. The story impressed me and I was convinced that he, too, sought a remedy to the mystery of the president's death thirty years ago.

> A young boy watched as five strong men struggled to load a seven-hundred-pound pig onto the back of a pickup truck. The pig was one of the largest on record at the time and it had received first-prize ribbons at the county fair. The men had no trouble unloading the pig when they arrived early that morning, but they had failed to consider how they would get the pig back onto the truck at the end of the day. The boy chuckled as he witnessed their attempts, but felt free to proposition the men. "For fifty cents," the young lad suggested, "I'll put that pig on the truck for you."
>
> The men were in no mood for the advice of a young boy, but one of them decided to take his offer. "Put the pig on the truck and I'll give you the fifty cents," replied the man. The others laughed persistently, yet without hesitation the young lad scurried over to the pig. Unafraid, he looked him right in the eye. Pushing the backside of the pig towards the rear end of the truck, the boy replaced the ramps that the men had previously used in their attempts to load the pig.
>
> A short distance away the boy spied a bushel basket. After picking up the basket and dumping its contents onto the ground, he quickly walked over to the pig and carefully placed the basket over the pig's head. To the astonishment of the men, the pig, being afraid of the basket, backed vigorously onto the truck.

Is the truth of the assassination beyond our capability or understanding? The ability to discern the truth is God-given and the grounds of our research is in the history of the event, not the abstract reasoning fostered by the dissenting views of the Warren Commission. Over the years many authors and historians have produced provisional works using as a basis for their work, prefabricated inconsistencies of their own creation. It is not that they chose to hide the truth as much as a prevailing pattern of plausible evidence encouraged their style. Through the Freedom of Information Act, many reports have been released and can account for the definitive style of penmanship utilized by many of the assassination researchers. These authors have produced what I call "straight talk," a style which rejects the Warren Commission's conclusion and continues to reflect the concern of government officials taking part in a cover-up conspiracy after the fact.

A New Direction

The American people have sincere commitment towards the survival of this great nation and with firm belief, I must conclude, based on the evidence that I have examined, that if the national security of this country is of greater value than the truth of John F. Kennedy's death ever reaching the people whom our elected government officials depend upon, then we have succumbed to a coward's view of democracy.

The coup d'etat suggested by many researchers, including Jim Garrison, covered many of the contradictions which emerged from the investigation into the assassination, but the litigations of the Warren Commission, the FBI, the justice department, and the researcher's guild, still to this day promote a misleading version of what happened in Dallas. Why? I differ to regard the assassination as being nothing more than it was, a deplorable act of treason which was both unpreventable and theatrically staged. It was a government revolution against the government, an egotistical team orchestrating an act of insurrection against the Kennedy administration with the hands of justice bound by an executive order governing the use of information collected by the Warren Commission.

"Report to me," was President Johnson's demand.

The evidence that came before the Commission was conclusive in that it not only suggested where to look for the assassin, it also was credible proof of the conspiracy once all the testimony was heard. Hard facts to the Warren Commission became unsubstantiated theories which could not be proven beyond a reasonable doubt. You decide just how much the Warren Commission knew. Was there credible evidence to link the assassination to a conspiracy? Why was there a subsequent cover-up? We can ponder the facts and raise more questions. We can seek out more evidence and remove the reasonable doubt, but can we as a nation be deprived our right to access the government's information and the officials whom we elect to serve us? I for one believe that the truth is known by many in Washington, yet the vast majority of our population has not been allowed to understand the mysterious facts about Dealey Plaza. You have the right to know!

Mirror of Doubt will allow you to see and by it you will retain the dignity that was robbed from you by our own elected representatives of the United States government. If who shot President John F. Kennedy still remains a question in your mind and you are convinced that Oswald did not act alone, look into *Mirror of Doubt* and ask yourself, who shot President Kennedy?

To regard the integrity of the American government as being a definitive instrument to mediate the truth is patriotic. However, for nearly thirty years we've witnessed many patriots use the "let the government take care of it" approach and it hasn't worked. The government has had more than ample time to reinvestigate the assassination of John F. Kennedy but has failed to release even the slightest detail. In 1976-1979, the House Select Committee on Assassinations looked briefly into the events of Dallas, but concluded nothing and sealed certain information for another fifty years.

Mirror of Doubt will disclose facts that have every relevancy in determining who shot President Kennedy. So with the facts as your guide, the mystery of the president's death can be solved. Remember this one thing; *The president's death was made a mystery—but it is not.* In the time it takes to read *Mirror of Doubt* you will learn why the truth of John F. Kennedy's death was covered up, who covered up the truth, and why for nearly three decades it has been kept from the American public. The conclusion is available. Search the facts. Listen to the evidence. Let the testimony of eyewitnesses be your guide and find the mirror of doubt. John F. Kennedy was an American, a father of two very young children, and your president. You have every right to know the circumstances surrounding his death, even though they may be controversial and the best kept government secret in the history of this nation.

The Motorcade

Two press busses

White House staff members' bus

Western Union vehicles

Admiral Burkley

Five dignitary cars—Mrs. Cabell—Congressman Ray Roberts
Vice-presidential follow-up car

Vice-presidential limousine
  Vice President Johnson, Mrs. Johnson, Senator Yarborough
  Rufus Youngblood, Patrolman Jacks

Secret Service agents—Presidential follow-up car
  Glen Bennett   George Hickey
  Dave Powers   Ken O'Donnell
  Paul Landis*   William McIntyre*
  John Ready*   Clint Hill*
  Emory Roberts   Sam Kinney (driver)
  *Indicates agents standing on running boards

Presidential limousine
  John F. Kennedy   Jacqueline Kennedy
  John Connally   Nellie Connally
  Roy Kellerman   William Greer

Chapter One

A Portfolio of Suspicion

On 29 November, 1963, one week after the death of President John F. Kennedy, by Executive Order No. 11130, President Lyndon Johnson appointed a commission to investigate the assassination. After ten months of reviewing facts, testimony, photographs, and motion pictures and listening to experts in the field of firearms, the Commission concluded its findings and reported to President Johnson in an eight-hundred-page report. This report became known as the Official Report of the President's Commission on the Assassination of President John F. Kennedy.

Ask anyone what they remember or what they know about the death of President Kennedy and you'll get nearly the same answer each time. Some know more than others, but for the most part they will tell you the government said, "Lee Harvey Oswald shot the president from the Texas Book Depository building, but they covered it up." You'll get other answers from those who believe more than Oswald participated in the event: the FBI; the Cubans backed by Castro; or even the mafia under close guard of a covert military-style operation carried out by the CIA or members of the Secret Service. The list is long, but the truth is most people have no idea who actually shot President John F. Kennedy while riding in an open limousine through the streets of Dallas on 22 November, 1963.

Circumstantial Evidence

Within minutes after the shooting, Texas law enforcement personnel emerged from the Book Depository boasting of finding a rifle and three empty cartridges behind a group of boxes near a sixth floor window. Less than two hours later, after the shooting of Dallas police officer, J.D. Tippit, Lee Harvey Oswald was arrested and charged with the murder of both Tippit and President Kennedy. The news spread like wildfire across the

1

country and by 5:00 P.M. Eastern time, nearly the entire country mourned the death of the president. Photographs of Oswald being escorted by the Dallas police and FBI officials were seen in living rooms across the nation and perhaps worldwide. The event shocked the entire world and immobilized America. The suspected assassin was in custody and to those who were investigating the assassination, the horrifying facts soon became clear.

Even the comforting news that a lone assassin was arrested could not relieve the tragic scars that struck the hearts of this nation's people. In the days that passed, tensions eased and the news of Oswald's untimely demise by Jack Ruby, a Dallas nightclub owner, provided further confirmation that justice was being served. Slowly and uneventfully the people of our country returned to their families and friends, finding little comfort from the news of Kennedy's death. Many felt that Jack Ruby was sent to silence Lee Harvey Oswald, but all too soon the tears began to slow and the death of the thirty-fifth president of the United States became history.

When the Dallas police retrieved the 6.5 millimeter Mannlicher-Carcano rifle from the sixth floor, the news of this find concentrated the attention of a few hundred or more spectators who heard the shots being fired. The majority of the witnesses heard only three shots, while the rest heard echoes. Yet many of these witnesses indicated in testimony that the sounds of the shots did not appear to come from the Depository building. This testimony, all too quickly, was regarded by the Commission as being controversial, as it contradicted the evidence found in the Depository. It was never released to the press or published in the Official Report.

One eyewitness, Senator Ralph Yarborough, a democrat from Texas, was riding in the vice-presidential limousine with Lyndon Johnson and three other witnesses only forty-five feet from the president as the shots rang out. The senator reported hearing three shots and reported to the Commission that he felt the shots were fired at a point to the right behind him. Though Yarborough's affidavit presented to the Commission indicates that the shots were fired from behind the presidential motorcade, this was not Yarborough's initial recollection of the event. As we will learn, based on the eyewitness accounts given by several other witnesses, (including Yarborough's first statement concerning the event), the sounds heard to the rear of the motorcade were more likely to be considered echoes off the high buildings.

Twisting Testimony of a Second Shot

According to reports Charles Brehm was standing on the south side of Elm Street with his five-year-old son, Joe. He reported hearing two shots. The first, Brehm reported, hit the president, as many other witnesses reported in close proximity to the presidential limousine. The moving motorcade approached the location where Brehm and his five-year-old son were standing. The presidential limousine had just passed when a second shot, Brehm recalled, hit the president in the head. However, the testimony of Charles Brehm remained uncorroborated from other eyewitness accounts.

Secret Service Agent Clint Hill and Mrs. Jacqueline Kennedy, were among several people who were the closest to the president when the shots were fired and they reported that the second shot hit President Kennedy in the head, but they heard *only* two shots. The testimony of eyewitnesses is crucial in any investigation and the Warren Commission's conclusion about three shots being fired included these testimonies. Can a "single bullet theory" be developed from these accounts alone?

It is my opinion, as well, that only three shots were fired but no shots missed. The evidence of the governor's reaction to the second shot is conducive to proving no shots missed, since only the president reacted to the first bullet fired and Governor Connally suffered from only one gunshot wound (re: testimony of William Newman and Senator Ralph Yarborough).

While Nellie and John Connally recalled a second shot striking the governor, Brehm said a second shot hit the president. Mrs. Kennedy and Clint Hill (the Secret Service agent who reached the car before it sped off to Parkland Memorial Hospital), on the other hand, heard *only two shots* and recalled that the second shot hit the president in the head. Emmett Hudson watched the motorcade pass and recalled hearing a fourth shot being fired as the car moved slowly down Elm Street. Yet Hudson reported the fourth shot after the head shot. Senator Yarborough heard only three shots and was very confident that only three shots were fired. Both James Altgens and William Newman recalled that the third shot hit only the president. Altgens said he was certain that the head shot was the last shot fired.

Though these accounts provide only a confusing reenactment of the shots fired in Dealey Plaza, credibility can be given to those accounts which are consistent to the medical evidence, trajectory analysis, testimony of other witnesses, and photographic evidence. The eyewitness descriptions of the wounds are specific in regard to the shots striking the men. However the exact positions of the men must then be recreated in order to truthfully account for these shots and the related testimony.

Table 1

Witness:	A	B	C	D	E	Distance to President
Mrs. Connally*	1	2	3			4 feet
John Connally*	1	2	3			3 feet
Mrs. Kennedy*	1	-	2			3 feet
Clint Hill*	1	-	2			15 feet
William Greer*	1	2	3			8 feet
Charles Brehm*	1	2	-			35 feet
Emmett Hudson*	1	2	3	4		60 feet
Bill Newman*	1	2	3			12 feet
James Altgens*	1	2	Last			35 feet
J.W. Foster	1	2	3			260 feet
Roy Kellerman*	?	?	3			6 feet
Glen Bennett *	1	2	3			30 feet
Clifton Carter	1	2	3			100 feet
Agent Youngblood	1	2	3			70 feet
Agent Ready	1	2	3			25 feet
Robert Jackson	1	2	3			300 feet
Sen. Yarborough	1	2	3			70 feet

*Actually saw bullets causing wounds.

Column *C* in Table 1 represents the sound of the shot which hit the president in the head at Frame 313 of the Zapruder film. The witnesses close enough to visualize which shot struck the president in the head are indicated by an asterisk. The numbers on the corresponding line of their name indicate which sound these witnesses related to the fatal head shot fired in Dealey Plaza and the total number of shots heard by each witness is represented by the last number in their line. (Example: Clint Hill heard only two shots and recalled the second shot hitting the president in the head.)

A review of the testimony and the eyewitness accounts provide a basis for determining just how many shots were fired and which bullet struck which man. The medical evidence provided the Commission with credible evidence that only one bullet caused the wounds sustained by Governor Connally and it was also determined medically by the examining surgeons at Bethesda Naval Hospital that President Kennedy was struck by only two bullets. The "single bullet theory" sponsored by the official report relies heavily upon Charles Brehm, Jackie Kennedy, and Clint Hill. Those that heard the first shot strike only the president, and the witness testifying to a third shot hitting the president in the head were presumably mistaken. There exists no other testimony to support the validity of the "single bullet theory."

4

Table 2

Witness	Total Shots	Testimony Reference
Mrs. Connally	3	2nd shot hit her husband in the back
John Connally	3	2nd shot hit him in his back
Mrs. Kennedy	2	2nd shot hit the president in the head
Clint Hill	2	2nd shot hit the president in the head
Roy Kellerman	1	saw the president react to the 1st shot
Will Greer	3	saw Connally fall after 2nd shot, 3rd hit Kennedy
Glen Bennett	3	3rd shot hit the president in head
James Altgens	3	3rd shot was last shot; hit the president
Charles Brehm	3	2nd shot hit the president
Emmett Hudson	3	3rd shot hit the president; then a 4th shot
Bill Newman	3	3rd shot hit the resident in the head

The Negatives

Headed by the chief justice of the United States, Earl Warren, the Commission's task was to review the testimony of witnesses and the evidence collected by the FBI and the Dallas authorities and report to President Johnson its conclusions. It is apparent from reading the Official Report that the Commission was not totally convinced that others weren't involved and it wasn't about to let you find out about it. One conclusion offered by the Commission failed to disclose the origin of the information it uncovered concerning the possible involvement of others, but it did indicate that certain information was left unsubstantiated. Evidence that perhaps would have revealed the true assassin's plot and a subsequent cover-up conspiracy was left unsubstantiated by the Commission.

The Report reads, "Because of the difficulty in proving negatives to a certainty, the possibility of others being involved with either Oswald or Ruby *cannot be rejected categorically*, but if there is any such evidence, it has been beyond the reach of all the investigative agencies and resources of the United States and has not come to the attention of this Commission."

The Commission regarded "negatives" as being evidence of a conspiracy, yet it rejected the possibility of others taking part in the assassination and simply closed the book on the president's death. The implications of certain evidence, which caused the Commission to conclude that others may have been involved, was not sufficient grounds to determine a conspiracy had taken place. This, however, should not have prevented it from concluding that Oswald could not have acted alone, nor prevented it from searching for the truth. Solving any murder case is a difficult task, but it is apparent that the Commission gave up on all possible leads thirty years ago.

What had the Commission hoped to prove by not following up on the testimony of eyewitnesses which indicated that the evidence found on the sixth floor of the Depository was suspicious? As we will learn, much of the eyewitness testimony reveals facts that would have lead the Commission to conclude that a conspiracy to kill President Kennedy had taken place and the gun found in the Depository was a plant, but the Commission regarded that testimony as being "negative." Where is the information that suggested others might have been involved with the president's death? What facts were relevant to understanding the events in Dallas and why were these facts kept from us?

The Commission spoke about the possibility of others being involved, but since it could not be proven, it chose to exonerate itself and convict Lee Harvey Oswald as a lone gunman. Oswald was dead and no one would be concerned as long as the government brought forth its decision.

It further concluded that there was "no evidence of a conspiracy either foreign or domestic."

This is just the beginning of a long list of conclusions offered by the Commission that indicates it knew more than it was willing to let out. What the Report would have you believe is that the Commission did the best job it could under the circumstances. The "negatives" the Report spoke of you will not find within the text of the Official Report and evidence that would tell a very different story of what happened in Dallas simply cannot be found in the Official Report given to President Johnson. It was locked away from the American people in a twenty-six-volume set of books containing this information. The Zapruder film, too, was held by the government for a period of five years following the assassination and the news media was forced to withhold showing the film.

What evidence did the Commission lack? What were the "negatives" experienced by the members of the Commission? Was there a conspiracy and did the Commission know about it? What were the difficulties? Was there a possibility of others being involved? Was the evidence out of the reach of the United States government? Why was the film kept from the American public? The potential of a new investigation exists today as it did thirty years ago.

Inconsistencies and Contradictions

The Warren Report, in my opinion, is an antagonistic compilation of the facts that neither suggests nor denies that a conspiracy took place. The Commission, in order to ease the tensions of a nation crippled by the death of a very distinguished young president, thwarted the facts to stifle future efforts to get at the truth. The Report centers around the supposed involvement of Lee Harvey Oswald, who denied any part in the assassination. In a later chapter we will review the evidence against Oswald, but first the contradictions surrounding the official version of the president's death must be addressed. What were the conclusions of the Commission and where did it get most of the information collected as a result of the investigation?

The evidence of the three shots being fired from behind the president, according to the Commission, was conclusive in that there was no evidence to suggest that the shots could have come from anywhere else.

The Commission said, "There is no credible evidence that the shots were fired from the Triple Underpass, ahead of the motorcade, or from any other location."

What is credible evidence? In legal definition it would mean that the Commission had reviewed no evidence that was considered either convincing or reliable. In other words it was impossible for anyone but an assassin stationed on the sixth floor of the Depository to fire the shots in Dallas that day! The entire report is scattered with brief explanations of how the Commission had all the facts, could reach no other conclusion, and would force its readers to draw the conclusion that the Commission was right about the shots being fired from the Depository.

Evidence of a Conspiracy

The Report also said, "The nature of the bullet wounds suffered by President Kennedy and Governor Connally and the location of the car at the time of the shots establish that the bullets were fired from above and behind the Presidential limousine."

What the Commission concluded is that the bullets entered both men from the rear when in fact their positions would have prevented rear entry wounds of this nature, since the medical reports from Parkland Hospital could have only precluded the possibility of the gunman being located on the sixth floor behind the motorcade causing these wounds.

President Kennedy's First Wound

According to FBI Agent Lyndal L. Shaneyfelt, the president's reaction to the first shot was clearly apparent in Frame 226 and barely apparent in Frame 225 of the Zapruder film. In a bullet trajectory study conducted by the FBI for the Warren Commission, it was determined that the distance from the president to the alleged assassin's window was 190.8 feet at Frame 226. The angle of trajectory from the president to the window was determined at 20.11 degrees. This would make it 65.6 feet vertically from ground level to the Depository sixth floor window.

Diagram 2

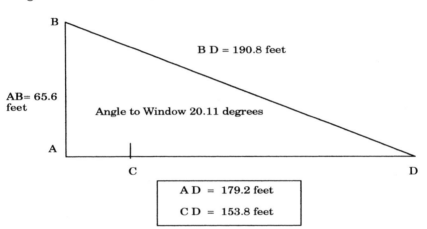

Trajectory Analysis of FBI at Frame 226

The Problem

According to the scientific medical evidence set forth by Dr. Humes and Dr. Boswell, the examining surgeons who performed the autopsy on President Kennedy, the wound of entrance from the first bullet was located high in his back, just left of the right shoulder blade. This bullet (striking no bones) *presumably* exited the Adam's apple, where it continued on to inflict the wounds sustained by the Texas governor.

While examining Frame 226 we find that the president was seated in an upright position facing forward. This bullet (traveling an estimated 1800 feet per second) entered at a 20 degree downward angle and then, according to the Commission, exited 5 inches higher, passing through the front of his throat. If John Kennedy had been putting on his shoe when the bullet entered his back, we could expect a trajectory of this nature. However, he was just completing his wave to the citizens scattered along the banks of the plaza.

The trajectory analysis conducted by the FBI for the Warren Commission proved that the bullet entrance discovered by Dr. Malcolm Perry in Parkland during his initial treatment of President Kennedy precluded the possibility of the upper back wound being related to the wound of entrance in the throat. As we can see for ourselves, it just wasn't possible for the wound found on Kennedy's throat to be caused by a bullet fired from above and behind the motorcade. Not only are the reported wounds inconsistent with the trajectory analysis of the FBI, the position of the president also prevented the bullet from entering low in a downward angle and then exiting high through the throat.

Though this may seem like a critical analysis of the official report, an inspection of the president's jacket and shirt reveals a bullet hole at the precise location where the autopsy surgeons reported an entrance wound. The wound locations and analysis provided by the autopsy report does not *verify* the theory of these wounds being related, but were assumed to be by Dr. Humes during the autopsy. No incisions were made to determine the path a bullet might have taken upon entering the president's back. If indeed this was a wound, no relationship can be given to positively relate this particular find, either medically or scientifically, to the wound found in the president's throat, it was not noted by the doctors at Parkland Hospital.

Diagram 3

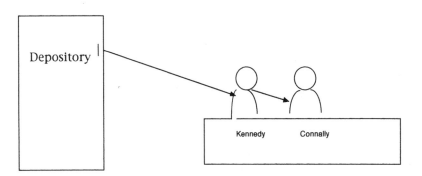

When Dr. Perry first examined and began treating President Kennedy, he disclosed to press reporters outside Parkland Hospital that there appeared to be an entrance wound just below the president's Adam's apple. These findings were inconclusive according to the Warren Commission, yet this bullet did not hit Governor Connally, seated directly in front of the president. The trajectory of the bullet was established by autopsy surgeons indicated above.

The rifle alleged by the Commission to have fired this shot was located high above the motorcade which proceeded down Elm Street. The bullet held a straight path of 20 degrees downward, entering the president's body at a point far below the presumed exit. No other wounds were reportedly found on the back of the president's body, which would have resulted in the hole Dr. Perry described as being an entrance wound below the Adam's apple.

President Kennedy's Fatal Head Wound

There can be no question as to the exact moment President Kennedy suffered his mortal head wound, nor discussion as to which frame of the Zapruder film details the bullet contacting the president's head or even the position of his head when the bullet made initial contact. According to the FBI it was determined that the distance to the rifle window was 265.3 feet and the angle to the rifle window at 15.21 degrees when the bullet entered the president's head. This was Frame 313 of the Zapruder film and it has been a primary focus of investigators since the Warren Commission concluded that Lee Harvey Oswald acted alone.

Diagram 4

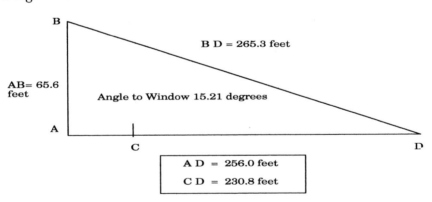

Trajectory Analysis of FBI at Frame 313

The Commission was quick to conclude that the first bullet which struck President Kennedy also struck the Texas governor, John Connally, upon exiting Kennedy's throat. However the third bullet became a bit of a puzzle. Regardless of the trajectory analysis of the first bullet, the Commission remained indecisive as to why the third bullet, which presumably exited the front portion of the president's head, did not strike other occupants of the limousine and was not found.

The Abraham Zapruder film was made available to the Commission. The Commission's staff and members reviewed the film, yet their conclusions remain contradictory to what we witness as the film is shown. (Note: If you have never seen the Abraham Zapruder film of the assassination, see Oliver Stone's movie *JFK*.) The detailed motion of the president's head being thrust violently backwards by the impact of the bullet is shocking but conclusive to a shot being fired from the front. When comparing Frame 313 of the Zapruder film to autopsy photos first released by David Lifton in his book *Best Evidence*, we can conclude that the Warren Commission was clearly wrong about the damage to the president's head and neck as well as the location of the gunman. Who fired the third shot in Dealey Plaza? Does the film contain credible evidence that would have supported a federal investigation?

Diagram 5

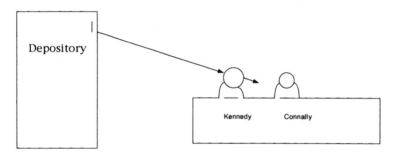

According to autopsy photos and the official autopsy report, the wounds sustained by President Kennedy were the result of a bullet being fired from above and behind the limousine. The violent motion of the president's head being propelled backwards was a result of the bullet's impact. The path of the bullet was established by the autopsy. However the position of the president's head was not taken into account. We cannot dispute the path the bullet took through the president based on the available medical evidence, yet the backwards motion of the president's head is conducive to determining that a shot was fired from the front and not the rear as recently concluded by the Journal of the American Medical Association.

Perhaps thirty years ago technology would not have allowed the Commission members to make an adequate determination through viewing the Zapruder film. If it is clear that the president's head moves violently backwards, then it is clear the third bullet came from the front. This one fact is what inspired David Lifton to continue his research of the assassination and pose serious questions as to the validity of the medical evidence reported from Bethesda and the observations of the Dallas doctors.

The Official Report also stated, "The Commission has found no evidence that anyone assisted Oswald in planning or carrying out the assassination, and has found no evidence that Oswald was involved with any person or group in a conspiracy to assassinate the President."

What this means to me (as a veteran researcher) is if there was a group conspiring to kill the president, then Oswald was not a part of it. The Zapruder film is clear and the facts contained in *Mirror of Doubt* may cause you to conclude the same. The fatal shot that struck the president came from the front, and if the Commission was not aware of this fact, it is possible that it simply did not know or could not determine if others were involved. But was it aware of the same contradictions that everyone has been concerned about for the past thirty years? The evidence before the Commission was credible and from that very same evidence the researchers of the assassination are learning that the Commission knew more than what it was willing to say and a conspiracy did take place.

When we see the word *conspiracy* it reminds us that the tragic death of the president was a premeditated plan implemented by more than one individual. Many times throughout the Report, the word *conspiracy* emerges, but attached to it we find *no evidence to suggest*. The Report said, "based on the evidence before the Commission." What about the evidence? Did it suggest a possible conspiracy?

Suppressing the Evidence

Found in the Book Depository, according to the Commission were, "the three cartridge cases and the cartridge case found in the rifle."

The Dallas police reported finding a live round in the gun, but later in the Report the Commission indicated that it was a cartridge case. To most who would normally be accustomed to the lingo used by firearms specialists, referring to an object as a *cartridge case* signifies that it contained no bullet. There is no real relevancy in pointing this out to you. The Report can be found to be both confusing and vague.

Senator Ralph Yarborough was very close to the building and was approximately forty-five feet behind the presidential limousine when the shots were fired. The senator reported, "There was one shot, a pause, another shot, a longer pause and then the third shot. The first two shots were fairly close together."

We could assume that the senator was accurate about what he heard and the Zapruder film can substantiate his claim; three shots and the first two being fairly close together. In the Depository building on the sixth floor, some seventy-five feet vertical to the motorcade, three spent 6.5 millimeter cartridge cases were found behind a group of boxes. When we consider the Commission's ruling that only three shots were fired, Senator Yarborough's account must be accepted as accurate considering his proximity to the Depository and the president's car, which provided him with firsthand knowledge of the event. The cartridges were found ejected behind a group of boxes which were presumably stacked for the purpose of establishing a rest for the rifle. It is entirely possible that after the cartridge cases were ejected from the gun, the gunman could have picked them up and discarded them next to the rifle. This would have required the officials to search for the remains left behind by the assassin and would have served no other purpose.

When a bolt action rifle similar to the one found in the Depository building ejects bullets, the spent cartridges are ejected back and to the right. The relevancy of the cartridges being found where they were does create controversy. It is possible, however, if the shots were fired in rapid succession, as they were, that a gunman could have quickly picked up the shells before rushing out of the building and discarded them behind the boxes. But were any shots fired from the building or did the three shots come from another location? Was there evidence overlooked by the Commission?

Speculation arose concerning the final shot that struck President Kennedy. The witnesses in the area of the presidential limousine reported seeing a puff of smoke in the area of a fence on the grassy knoll. This grassy embankment lies to the right of the motorcade where many witnesses began to run to after seeing the President's head thrust violently backwards. This fact was determined by the Warren Commission as being inconclusive. However the puff of smoke reported by the witnesses does raise the question of a firearm being discharged from the knoll. It is my opinion, based on other facts relevant to this study, that the witnesses saw what they saw, but it did not relate to a firearm being discharged from the knoll. In the days of Daniel Boone and Davy Crockett, one would witness just such an effect. Modern firearms, however, do discharge a visible residual of ignited gunpowder when they are fired, but the effect is not quite as dramatic as the conclusion offered by the witnesses.

What made the witnesses flee towards the grassy knoll area after the shot struck the president in the head? The Zapruder film is hard evidence that a third shot could have come from the knoll area, though it was the motion of the president's head that resulted in the spectators moving towards the area of the knoll. The evidence contained in the Zapruder film substantiates the reactions of the people who raced towards a probable location of a gunman because of the backwards motion of the president's head and not the puff of smoke in front of the witnesses standing on the south side of Elm Street. What relevant facts were dismissed by the Warren Commission? How many shots were fired in Dealey Plaza? Was there more than one gunman? We know that Senator Yarborough was one of the eyewitnesses who reported hearing three shots and three cartridges cases were found with a rifle on the sixth floor of the Book Depository.

The Smell of Gunpowder

As we continue to learn more about the assassination, the "negative file" will grow and the Commission will continue to dismiss relevant information concerning the event. We will review testimony of witnesses who reported smelling gunpowder on the grounds of the plaza in the area of the motorcade as the shots rang out. We will learn that a nearly whole bullet was found in Parkland Hospital and perhaps we will need a fourth cartridge case for this bullet. We will also have an opportunity to examine the very same evidence that the Commission used to determine Oswald's sole guilt and sponsor its theory of a single bullet striking both men.

The Rules of Evidence

The Zapruder film, according to the Commission, was not conclusive proof that a gunman could have been located anywhere, except above and behind the presidential limousine. Why didn't the Commission conclude that a third shot could have been fired from somewhere other than the Depository building? Who convinced it that the third shot came from behind? Were there other medical findings at Parkland Hospital which indicated that the president was shot from the front, not from behind? If we can conclude by the motion of the president's head that the third shot struck the president from the front, we should also, from the medical evidence and the position of the president's head at the time of impact, determine the trajectory of the bullet and the location of the gunman who fired the third and fatal shot. Would this have been sufficient grounds to determine where the fatal shot came from? Was there other evidence disregarded by the Commission that provided compelling proof that the third and fatal shot came from the front? What did it know?

The availability of the evidence and the simplistic course of events which transpired after the presidential motorcade reached Parkland Hospital provided the Commission with proof of a conspiracy. Once at Parkland Hospital, the facts became clear. If the Warren Commission had, however, ruled that a third shot was fired from the grassy knoll area or any other location consistent with the backwards motion of the president's head, the federal government would have seized jurisdiction over the assassination. History indeed would have changed and the lone gunman "single bullet theory" would have been dismissed as a cover-up attempt made by the conspirators and not by our own government officials.

The Report states, "There was no Federal criminal jurisdiction over the assassination of President Kennedy. Had there been reason to believe that the assassination was the result of a conspiracy, Federal jurisdiction could have been asserted; it has long been a Federal crime to conspire to injure any Federal officer, on account of, or while he is engaged in, the lawful discharge of the duties of his office. Murder of the President has never before been covered by Federal law, however, so that once it became reasonably clear that the killing was the act of a single person, the State of Texas had exclusive jurisdiction."

If we can imagine America as a democratic society, we can hardly assume that the Commission members had the best interest of the country at heart when they so eagerly gave up solving the president's death in Dallas. The objective was to keep the facts from the American people. The "grassy knoll assassin theory" was effectively dismissed by the Warren Commission and the evidence of the president's head thrust backwards was deemed inconclusive to other findings. Many researchers have regarded the assassination as a "blue ribbon" cover-up construed by official reports which released only facts that would have substantiated Oswald's guilt. Though the grassy knoll was suggested to be the location of a gunman, there was no credible evidence to convince the Commission otherwise.

Was there evidence of a conspiracy even though there was no credible evidence to suggest that shots were fired anywhere other than the Book Depository? Was the movement of the president's head as the bullet made contact conclusive? It inspired many researchers to look into resolving the president's death, but the Commission in its infinite wisdom chose to hide the truth from us and keep the facts and evidence locked away in secret files. Since it found no evidence, the Commission ruled that the third shot came from behind. Is that the way to conduct a criminal investigation? Where was the gunman? Who fired the third shot? Was there testimony which indicated the presence of a second gunman in Dealey Plaza? Has all the medical evidence been released?

A Chain Is As Strong As Its Weakest Link

Evidence of a conspiracy was unlikely to reach the Warren Commission because of the involvement of the Dallas police department and the federal government's willingness to disregard conclusive proof of a conspiracy. The jurisdiction remained with the Dallas authorities, and the federal agencies were mere pawns of the Warren Commission. Even the suspicions offered by President Johnson after the Commission had completed its report failed to promote a new investigation into the allegations of a conspiracy. The Commission would have us believe that the report was a concise reflection of the events and that no cover-up existed.

The efforts of researchers in the past have caused the release of some information. However the bulk of the text has been sealed by the House Select Committee until the year 2029, at a point in time when all who were present at Dealey Plaza when the president was assassinated will have died. This information would add to the preponderance of evidence and prove beyond a question of doubt that the Commission, the FBI and President Johnson knew who shot President Kennedy and why! We must stop and consider now why the government will not release certain information about the assassination. What does it know that it is afraid to tell us? Have you learned of new evidence that may cause you to believe that all of the shots were not fired from the Depository?

The Witnesses Were Wrong?

Eyewitness testimony played a small role in the definitive conclusions of the Commission. The weight of the evidence was placed heavily upon the role of Lee Harvey Oswald, which strongly suggested he was the lone gunman. Much of the testimony given by eyewitnesses could not be accepted because of the inconsistencies which emerged after the testimonies were compiled. From these accounts, it was determined that only three shots were fired, even though much of this testimony did not substantiate the shots coming from the Depository. The basis for this is that the acoustical design of the plaza preempted locating the origin of the shots.

While some witnesses heard only three shots, others heard four. Some heard only two and yet others heard as many as six shots. Experts have regarded this testimony as being conclusive, in lieu of the fact that the echoes from the various buildings would have caused certain witnesses to hear more than three shots and to visualize actual bullets striking by the sounds of the echoes of previous shots. Too, with the shock and trauma of the event, the accuracy of testimony relied heavily on the location of each witness and what they saw or experienced when they heard the shots being fired. As a result the eyewitnesses closest to the motorcade did not testify before the Commission and many of these accounts never reached the American public. When we keep in mind that echoes are sound impulses which are transmitted back towards the source after bouncing off dense barriers (such as buildings, mountains, etc.), certain witnesses heard shots coming from just west of the Depository where sound impulses would have had a great deal of trouble finding such barriers.

If all the shots were indeed fired from the Depository, how is it that the echoes were heard in an area (the open plaza) which is not conducive to accepting sound impulses?

The Multitude of a Few

The Commission dramatized the assassination in an attempt to convince the American public that thousands of people witnessed the shots being fired, whereby the accounts could not be sorted out. The information gathered on Lee Harvey Oswald was accepted primarily on the basis of the gun being found and a few witnesses whose recorded testimony indicated that the shots came from the building. After the gun was found, even those who didn't see anything could have easily imagined themselves being questioned by authorities. What would you have reported after having knowledge that a gun and three empty cartridge cases were found in the Depository and that one of its employees was reported missing?

The validity of the information contained in the Official Report can be questioned, as it does not offer the clarity one can expect from law professionals issuing a final report on an assassination of a president. How soon in its investigation did the Commission ascertain that Oswald acted alone? The Commission continued to dismiss accounts that suggested a different event taking place and it is clear from reading the official version, the complexity of the assassination offered numerous alternatives.

The Creation of Evidence

It was determined that a bullet found on Governor Connally's stretcher in Parkland Hospital was fired from the gun found on the sixth floor of the Depository to the exclusion of all other weapons. The Commission created a gray area concerning this stretcher bullet, which had wrought confusion and uncertainty. The researchers of the assassination have regarded this bullet as a joke, in that it could not have been fired from the gun without sustaining some damage. One look at the bullet and you will agree that it could not have been fired from the gun found on the sixth floor and still be found in the condition in which it was found. This bullet and the theory issued by Arlen Specter, chief council investigator to the Commission, will be discussed in a later chapter, but we will discuss briefly the *stretcher bullet*.

The three cartridge cases indicated three shots fired and only three shots were heard. If one bullet missed both men, another struck both Governor Connally and the president, and a final bullet struck only President Kennedy, a fourth bullet would then become the *stretcher bullet*. The condition of the bullet was what one can expect if it were simply pulled out of the cartridge case without being fired. It was found in Parkland Hospital on the stretcher of Governor Connally. The credibility of what the Commission reported as the fourth cartridge case, in lieu of three shots heard and the *stretcher bullet*, raises questions of a conspiracy to confuse the event. It is my opinion that the *stretcher bullet* was planted after the assassination, as evidence of a conspiracy and a lone gunman.

The Report regarded the bullet as nearly whole, and it was this bullet that raised controversy of a conspiracy.

How could a bullet traveling at a rate of 2000 feet per second remain in the condition in which it was found in Parkland Hospital? If four shots were fired, why did the Commission conclude that only three were fired? From the credible testimony, how many shots were heard in Dealey Plaza?

One missed, one struck the president and the governor, another struck only the president and the fourth: "The nearly whole bullet found on Governor Connally's stretcher at Parkland Memorial Hospital." If the whole bullet was found on the stretcher, was it fired from the sixth floor window along with the other three bullets? Was it possible to dismiss the fact that a fourth bullet showed up in the condition it did without suggesting that a conspiracy to confuse the event was taking place? It couldn't have just exited the president's body and rolled out onto John Connally's stretcher at Parkland Hospital.

The *stretcher bullet* was placed in the Commission's "negative file" and no concise conclusion was offered by the Commission as to the existence or relevancy of the bullet or its condition. Again this does not reflect the type of investigation the American public would expect concerning the assassination of its president.

Commission Exhibit #399—The Stretcher Bullet
The bullet reasoned by the Warren Commission as the bullet which caused all the wounds sustained by both President Kennedy and Texas governor, John Connally. (Photo courtesy of Assassination Archives and Research Center.)

Commission Exhibit #856—The Cadaver Bullet
This bullet was test fired into the wrist bone of a cadaver by the Commission, proof enough that the stretcher bullet was planted in the cover-up conspiracy attempt. (Photo courtesy of Assassination Archives and Research Center.)

Passing the Buck

The Commission remained indecisive when ascertaining which bullet struck Governor Connally and indicated it wasn't important to determine exactly which bullet struck the governor.

The Report reads, "Although it is *not necessary to any essential findings* of the Commission to determine just which shot hit Governor Connally, there is very persuasive evidence from the experts to indicate that the same bullet which pierced the President's throat also caused Governor Connally's wounds."

I like to ask, what was the Commission looking for if it wasn't essential to determine which shot struck Governor Connally? A professional botch job or what? How could the Commission hope to prove that the shots were fired from behind the president without concluding beyond a question of a doubt which of the three shots heard actually struck Governor John Connally of Texas, seated in front of the president?

The Commission later indicated that a difference of opinion arose concerning which bullet struck Governor Connally. Though the clarity of this determination is vague, it continues to resemble the obscure method of reporting used by the Commission.

The Report reads, "But there is no question in the mind of any member of the Commission that all the shots that caused the President's and Governor Connally's wounds *were* fired from the sixth floor window of the Texas School Book Depository."

If the report reads correctly, the Commission illogically represented its conclusion. The Commission knew that if the first bullet struck the president from behind, it would have had to hit Governor Connally, but since it did not and the Commission had obtained no evidence to substantiate this fact, it conceded to the "single bullet theory." If the Commission had examined the Zapruder film under the pretense of the shots being fired from the front or any other location, the answers would have been found. Not all of the Commission members were convinced.

Why wouldn't the Commission have speculated, for the purpose of investigating, that the gun and bullets were planted and that there may have been an assassin in another location who could have easily planted the gun or had the gun and shells planted to aid in the assassination attempt? It seems like a plausible concept. While reviewing the Zapruder film, the Commission noted that the shot that struck both Governor Connally and the president presumably occurred while both men were hidden behind the Stemmons Freeway sign. This sign obstructed the view of Abraham Zapruder during the filming of the motorcade for about two seconds. When the limousine emerged, Governor Connally was unharmed and the president began raising his right hand.

Contrary to the Commission's decision that both men were struck while hidden behind the Stemmons Freeway sign, the FBI reported that the president did not show signs of being struck until Frame 226, at a point in the film when both men had already emerged. It was suggested by the Commission that it could not substantiate which shot struck the men, but it was probable that the first shot missed. Yet according to eyewitness testimony, the "first shot fired caused the president to clutch at his throat." and Governor Connally turned to his left in response to this shot. This is an indication, at least, that the first shot did not miss the president. What about the governor? As previously discussed, the Commission wasn't interested in which shot struck Governor Connally. It felt that it didn't make a difference, but concluded that it had persuasive evidence that the bullet that hit the president also hit the governor.

The Commission refused to argue this point and the testimony of John Connally and other eyewitnesses, was deemed controversial by the Commission and determined to be inconclusive. The Commission concluded that the first bullet would have had to hit the governor if it had come from behind and a second shot, if it had hit Connally, could not have been fired from the sixth floor window of the Depository because there wasn't enough time in between the shots and it did not hit the president. Therefore it determined the second shot missed both men and Governor Connally was wrong about hearing the first shot and not being hit by it, thus justifying its "no conspiracy theory."

How would the Commission know anything about the time in between shots if it didn't know which bullet struck the governor. The Commission previously indicated that it could not determine the position of John Connally when he was shot, so what would time have to do with it anyway? A second shot being fired from a different location would have been proof of a second gun, not a lone assassin firing at the president. It seems that any evidence that would have suggested the involvement of others was determined to be invalid very quickly and it was better for the Commission to not know which shot hit the governor.

The Politics of the Investigation

The Commission's attitude towards examining the evidence was biased in that its report provided compelling evidence of Oswald's guilt but failed to attract the need to produce concise reflections of the truth based on the facts. The Commission members were apprehensive about determining the applicability of certain unsubstantiated claims that they themselves uncovered. Throughout the entire report, the Commission shuttled information from one theory to another and in the end issued vague conclusions. The violent motion of the president's head, the *stretcher bullet*, the possibility of others involved, the eyewitness testimony, the location of the three shots heard, the nature of the bullet wounds (rear entry), the smell of gunpowder, and the persuasive evidence of the single bullet striking both men are just a few of the many inconsistencies surrounding the conclusions offered by the Commission. The Zapruder film, too, does not substantiate the conclusions offered by the Commission.

The Commission again provided its report with incompleteness when it spoke of not being able to re-create certain moments of the assassination.

Chapter Three of the Official Report reads, "The alignment of the points of entry was only indicative and not conclusive that one bullet hit both men. The exact position of the men could not be re-created; thus, the angle could only be approximated."

Let's reopen the investigation. The exact position of the men can be created, and the alignment of the points of entry indicates that it would have been impossible for a single bullet to strike the president and Governor Connally when we compare the actual medical evidence and the Zapruder film. It would also prove beyond a question of a doubt that the shots which struck the president could not have been fired from the Depository where the gun and three empty shells were recovered.

It is a wonder that the Commission was able to conclude anything. When providing analysis in regard to the bullet that struck Governor Connally, the Commission obviously regarded the Zapruder film as "not conclusive enough to re-create the assassination of the President." What is the reason for not using the film as a basis for re-creating the assassination? Does the film detail the reactions of the president and the governor when the bullets struck? Did the FBI not report that President Kennedy clearly reacted to the bullet in Frame 226 of the Zapruder film? The backwards motion of the president's head, as well, is certainly visible in the film, as was the president's reaction to the bullet that transited his windpipe.

The governor said that the first bullet did not hit him. If the reactions of the president are visible in the Zapruder film, what about the reaction of Governor Connally when the first shot was fired? Can it not be determined by viewing the film why the first bullet did not hit Governor Connally? I believe Governor Connally! The first bullet didn't hit the Texas governor because he wasn't in the line of its trajectory. Obviously, the Commission's ability to produce a concise report was limited severely by the availability of resources. The nation was in the process of sending a man to the moon, yet the Commission was unable to examine the Zapruder film under the pretense of the shots being fired from somewhere else to determine which shots hit the president and the position of Governor Connally when he was shot. People who live in glass houses shouldn't live in glass houses.

Much of the evidence that came before the Warren Commission was torn apart and put back together. The Commission examined a given piece of information by "what if's" and "or if's." When it finally concluded what probably had happened, it would return once again with a "but if." This investigative style is seen throughout the entire Official Report. My intentions are not to criticize the report but to interpret the findings of the Commission as they relate to the facts available to it at the time and to relay to the American public that its government did a lousy job investigating John Kennedy's death, but a terrific job of covering it up. It is clear by all the "negatives" experienced by the Commission that it knew more than it was willing to admit to and presumably had no intentions of justifying the shooting of the president or revealing the "negatives" to us. What the Commission didn't want you to know, it didn't tell you and it wasn't about to prove it to itself either.

The Commission spent hundreds of exhausting hours preparing the Official Report, yet certain members of the Commission have regarded the researchers of the assassination of President Kennedy, who have spent nearly their entire lives researching his death, as incompetent critics. That's sort of the pot calling the kettle black. In my opinion if the Commission members continue to regard the evidence as being inconclusive, they are incriminating themselves as taking part in a government cover-up conspiracy to keep the truth from us. If this is their wish, then so be it.

Enough Is Enough

The evidence that the Commission used to conclude that Lee Harvey Oswald acted alone is the very same evidence that the researchers are using to conclude otherwise. The members of the Warren Commission have not obtained complete ownership rights to the facts and evidence pertaining to the death of President Kennedy, nor can their report be regarded as the gospel. Human nature seeks the essence of truth beyond any evasive technique used to fortify its concealment. If the Commission members voluntarily choose to stand on their decision, then publishing the truth will be left to the researchers and the Commission's part in the cover-up conspiracy is sure to be exposed.

The researchers are not alone, but they stand on truth and have made every effort to ensure an adequate transition of facts to the government and the public. It is imperative, but not essential, that any preestablished lines of prosecution remain open so as not to inhibit pending criminal investigations, court proceedings, or the right of individuals to a fair trial. A similar proclamation to this was issued by the Warren Commission thirty years ago, but to this day has only preempted authors and researchers of the assassination from telling the whole story. *Mirror of Doubt* will not be a part of controlling the usage of facts relevant to its readers understanding the truth. If the evidence proves to be credible and provides insight into the assassination, then the undertaking of this book will be successful and the facts will be disclosed.

The intelligence of the Commission can be accepted, but the destiny of its conclusions can no more remain a guiding interest for the security of this nation. The people are strong and the vision of democracy stronger, and a government which operates in seclusion is but a group of individuals who oppose the structure of a republic. Our government has a story to tell and it's not about a lone gunman and three empty shells found on the sixth floor of the Texas School Book Depository.

Researching the assassination of President Kennedy requires a dedication which surpasses the ability and time available to the average citizen. You have the right to learn about the facts that the Commission and your government chose to keep from you. They'll tell you that the facts are available for everyone to review, but are they? Much of the testimony was recorded in a twenty-six-volume set of books, which may or may not be found in your public library system. Today these are reference materials and are not allowed to leave the library. The evidence in part, not in whole, was kept from us. But they knew.

Here's how!

Chapter Two

A Prologue of Conspiracy

The photographic evidence reviewed by the Warren Commission was examined by the FBI in various reenactments designed to provide insight into the assassination. The FBI and the Commission worked hand in hand throughout the entire investigation into the president's death; uncovering a considerable amount of material which remained out of the reach of Texas law enforcement investigators. The photographic evidence pertaining to this case became a subject of intense study by researchers of the assassination, whereby many had proven that photo alterations had taken place, perhaps even before the assassination attempt occurred.

As with any investigation, photographs taken during a crime provide law enforcement officials with firsthand knowledge of the scene which might otherwise never be re-created. By the time the Commission had obtained photos taken on the day of the assassination, many had already reached the public through associated press wire photo releases. The Dallas police department had issued a statement regarding any and all photographs taken that day and requested they be brought to the Dallas police station for the purpose of obtaining leads into the assassination. Much of this information was not returned to the rightful owners and no compensation was warranted by the government or the state of Texas to these people for their photographs and motion picture films. The photographs and motion pictures taken in Dealey Plaza on 22 November, 1963 add to the preponderance of the evidence collected by the government. However the Commission failed to recognize that certain photos implicated a conspiracy.

Indisputable Evidence

The Warren Commission developed numerous picture exhibits which were later entered and numbered. When the Commission began developing its conclusions, each relevant exhibit was incorporated into the Report by a number for easy access.

The Abraham Zapruder film which provided the Commission with startling details of the assassination was placed into exhibit in two forms: first a copy of the original 8 millimeter film and then still frames of the entire sequence. Each frame was numbered beginning with number one as the presidential limousine began its decent down Elm Street and ending several seconds after the fatal head shot as the limousine entered the Triple Underpass. The detail of the Zapruder film is both shocking and disturbing. Those who have reviewed the film can relate to the vivid account of the final shot which struck President Kennedy and resulted in his death. The visibility of the president's head being thrust backwards in the film is equivalent to the reaction one would see watching a boxing match. When they throw a punch in the ring, there aren't many spectators who see an opposite reaction. This reproduction of the assassination, the Abraham Zapruder film did not convince either the Commission or the House Select Committee on Assassinations which convened in late 1970s. These agencies of our government examined the film, but both failed to elaborate on their findings or conclude that the president was shot from the front.

The autopsy photographs, when compared to the Zapruder film, confirm beyond reasonable doubt that the fatal shot which struck the president in the head was clearly the result of a frontal assault by a gunman whose location and identity remains to this day undisclosed by the government. The Commission's report reflects that there was no credible evidence available (including photographs) which would substantiate the shots being fired from any location other than the Book Depository building and the Commission members never reviewed the autopsy photographs during their lengthy investigation into the president's death; which would have raised many questions concerning the validity of the autopsy conducted in Bethesda, Maryland.

Probably a Conspiracy

The evidence of the assassination, based largely upon the photographs and motion pictures taken by witnesses at the scene, promotes the "conspiracy theory" accepted by the researchers. The House Select Committee in 1979 concluded that there was probably a conspiracy, but failed to substantiate the claims of the Zapruder film, the autopsy photos, and other photographic evidence examined by the Commission. The researchers have done a better job investigating the assassination than the Warren Commission and the House Select Committee on Assassinations.

The facts cannot be dismissed, yet two government investigations have failed to conclude or continue to investigate the implications of the photographic evidence. It should be apparent to most people that the government simply does not want the American public or the world to learn the shocking details of John Kennedy's assassination that it uncovered in 1964 and again in 1979. The facts surrounding 22 November, 1963 can be found and the shocking truth revealed. The photographic evidence holds the secret to resolving the doubt of a conspiracy taking place, but the government which serves us will not recognize the need for this information to come out. Perhaps even after *Mirror of Doubt* reaches the public, you will be forced to believe the Official Report.

Foreword for this Chapter

The purpose of this chapter is to expose the James Altgens photograph which appears in Commission Exhibit #900 as being one of the most conclusive findings which determines that a cover-up conspiracy did in fact take place and prove beyond a reasonable doubt that the Warren Commission and the FBI knew this photo was altered. This chapter of *Mirror of Doubt* requires each reader to examine several photographs taken the day of the assassination, compare the photos, and draw a simple conclusion. Were the photos altered or are they genuine?

It is my opinion that the Altgens photo, which appears in Commission Exhibit #900, was in fact altered and the FBI knew it. It isn't clear if the FBI informed the Commission that this photo was altered by reading the Commission's report, but it is clear that the Commission regarded the photo as being suspicious in nature and knew which frame of the Zapruder film corresponded to this photo.

For the purpose of study, I'll remind the reader that detecting photo alterations is very complicated. The variations will be spelled out as simply as possible, but try not to spend a great deal of time in this chapter. You can come back. Initially because of the mind boggling aspects of photo alterations, I had intended to place this chapter at the end of the book, but its relevancy to a conspiracy taking place has historical value here. Regardless of who shot the president, others were involved in the cover-up and this photograph proves just that!

One Picture—Three Photos

There were three versions of the Altgens photo. The first version, which can be located in the *New York Daily News* of 23 November, 1963, appeared in newspapers across the country the day after the assassination. The Altgens photo became known as Commission Exhibit #900 and played a decisive role in determining when the first shot was fired and if the president and Governor Connally had sustained wounds at the time this photo was taken.

The second version (also cropped) appeared (uncropped) in the *Saturday Evening Post* of 14 December, 1963. The Warren Commission received and placed into exhibit a cropped photo of the second version, but when comparing it to the first version, startling differences appear! The third version was an uncropped, exact replica of the negative containing the entire scene shot by the camera. The Warren Commission received a copy of the uncropped version when Senator Ralph Yarborough of Texas submitted a written affidavit at the request of Commission staffers on 10 July, 1964 detailing, in part, his recollection of the event with the uncropped photo attached. This became known as the Yarborough Exhibit. The Warren Commission did not publish the uncropped version in its report, but it is clear that it had the photo in its possession.

The photo alterations can be detected by examining all three photos together, yet there can be no question as to the validity of the photos as being one in the same. By comparing the witnesses in the background to the moving cars, each photo aligns perfectly with the background. Since the cars were moving and the Altgens photo was a still shot, it would have been impossible to snap an additional photo and have the people remain vertical to the positions of the car. *The car moved, but the people and the cameraman did not.* The conclusion that all three photos are the same picture is correct. The inconsistencies, which provide us with evidence that this photo was altered, appear when comparing the photos to the Zapruder film and attempting to determine which frame of the film corresponds to the photo.

Tunnel Vision

What are the variations if the photo was altered? Why was it altered? What frame of the Zapruder film corresponds to the Altgens photo?

The Commission's report reads, "James W. Altgens, a photographer in Dallas for the Associated Press, had stationed himself on Elm Street opposite the Depository to take pictures of the passing motorcade. Altgens took a widely circulated photograph which showed President Kennedy reacting to the first of the two shots which hit him....According to Altgens, he snapped the picture 'almost simultaneously' with a shot which he is confident was the first one fired. Comparison of his photograph with the Zapruder film, *however,* revealed that Altgens took his picture at approximately the same moment as frame 255 of the movie, 30 to 45 frames (approximately 2 seconds) later than the point at which the President was shot in the neck."

When comparing the Zapruder film to the Altgens photograph, the Commission concluded that the corresponding frame of the film was Frame 255. The basis of this determination was that Mrs. Kennedy had placed her white-gloved hand on the president's forearm, while Secret Service Agent Roy Kellerman could be seen facing forward, but slightly to his left. Also as President Kennedy clutched at his throat, Governor Connally had turned to his right and was facing the car door when Frame 255 was taken. These features of the Altgens photograph do appear to compare with Frame 255, yet when examining the *uncropped version* of the photo, the rest of the elements of this picture do not remain consistent to what should be seen. If Frame 255 were the corresponding frame, would not everything else in the photo remain consistent?

The Commission's study of the Altgens photograph compared to the Abraham Zapruder film was inaccurate. In my opinion, the FBI knew it and so did the Warren Commission. Although the Warren Commission received the uncropped version nearly six months later when Senator Yarborough submitted his affidavit, it would have clearly had to have the uncropped photo in its possession prior to creating Commission Exhibit #900, which includes a cropped version of the photo. Why did the Commission crop it?

It is understandable why the press would used cropped photos, but with the Warren Commission it becomes a bit of a puzzle. What prevented the Commission from publishing the entire photo in its Official Report? Did certain parts of the photo seem peculiar to the Commission?

Photograph by AP Photographer

Photograph from Reenactment

Commission Exhibit #900
The FBI reenacted the taking of the Altgens photo for the purpose of determining the location of the president's car when the photo was taken. Note the close proximity of the "stone pillar" to the surveyors standing in the background. (Photos courtesy of AP/Wide World, James Altgens, and Assassination Archives and Research Center.)

FBI Reenactment of the Photo

The FBI reenacted the taking of the Altgens photo and it became part of Commission Exhibit #900. In this exhibit both the Altgens photo and the FBI reenactment appear and provided conclusive evidence to determining *the exact location* of the presidential limousine when the Altgens photo was taken. What evidence is there that the FBI and perhaps the Commission knew that the photo had been altered? How can we prove the photo was altered? Did the photo correspond to Frame 255 of the Zapruder film, as the Commission indicated?

In the following chapters, we will learn that by Frame 255 of the Zapruder film, two shots had been fired, making it inconceivable for the Altgens photo to have corresponded to Frame 255 because of the location of the president's car at the time the photo was taken. Altgens reported that his photo was taken as a result of hearing the first shot, and testified that the third shot struck President Kennedy in the head. (Frame 313) Therefore Frame 255 would not be the frame anyway.

In the Altgens photo (See Commission Exhibit #900), the presidential limousine's front tire has passed slightly by one of the several painted lines on Elm Street. The FBI, during its reenactment, then placed its car on the very same street stripe and took a picture. Compare the two by taking an additional picture from where Abraham Zapruder was standing and we have the corresponding frame of the Zapruder film. It's that simple! Or at least it should have been.

As Plain as the Nose on Your Face

There are several discrepancies contained in the three versions of the Altgens photo, and by comparing these photos to the Zapruder film, we find that certain objects have been added to the Altgens photo, where in the Zapruder film, they are simply not there. (This doesn't mean that they never existed. It simply means these objects are not where they are supposed to be.) This indicates that the photograph contained superimposed images which were cut and pasted onto a base negative.

The three copies of the Altgens photo you will examine here can be regarded as being similar in context to the people and buildings in the background, but photo alterations exist and can be easily detected once we determine which frame of the Zapruder film corresponds to the Altgens photo. When this is achieved, we can completely examine this evidence, compare the photos to each other, and draft a general consensus of the inconsistencies we find. We will be able to place the president's car in the proper location and conclude beyond a reasonable doubt which Zapruder frame corresponds to the Altgens photograph. Is it Frame 255 as the Warren Commission suggested? You decide!

Head Start Conspiracy

In the first version of the Altgens photo, (A), notice the windshield area above the white glove on Mrs. Kennedy's hand and a defined line of space over the top of Governor Connally's head. The area above the glove is gray in texture and the clothing worn by the spectators in the background is not visible. The president's face resembles a shadow and his head looks more like a tiny black blob. The detail of the white glove worn by Mrs. Kennedy is clear and there appears to be a slight jog in the president's jacket sleeve. The outline of the president's shoulder is not visible above the wrist and white glove. The president's hand and wrist are perfectly horizontal to the rest of the picture, while his head is positioned much lower than Governor Connally's.

The area above the president's head is also gray and a large gap appears. Agent Roy Kellerman, seated on the passenger side of the limousine, is facing left center. Notice, too, the motorcycle next to the presidential limousine. It appears that it is about two to five feet from the car, but in direct line with Governor Connally, and its operator is looking at the president. This version of the Altgens photo did not reach the Warren Commission, but if it did it was not published in the Report as one of its exhibits. There seems to be little detail concerning the interior view of the limousine, but it is clear that Mrs. Kennedy's hand has reached the president's forearm.

New York Daily News, **Saturday, 23 November, 1963**

Photo A

Above is the first version of the Altgens photo that appeared in newspapers across the country the day after the assassination. Note the closeness of the motorcycle riding adjacent to the president's car in the left hand margin of the photo. It appears that it is very close to the car and the driver is looking back at President Kennedy. Compare this photo to a blow-up of the one found in Commission Exhibit #900. (Photo use courtesy of AP/Wide World Photo.)

Saturday Evening Post, **14 December, 1963**

Photo B

Above the second version of the Altgens photo which appeared in the Saturday Evening Post of 14 December, 1963 shows clarity which cannot be found in the first version. Again note the closeness of the motorcycle riding right rear of the presidential limousine. Without examination of the uncropped version, a look through the windshield portion of the limousine tells us that this photo compares to about Frame 255 of the Zapruder film. (Photo courtesy of AP/Wide World Photo.)

Clear Up the Mistakes

In photo (B), notice that the view of the spectators through the limousine windshield has improved with clarity. Where photo (A) showed a defined area of space above the governor's and the president's heads, it has been blackened out in the second version. The president's jacket sleeve does not contain the jog seen in photo (A) and the jacket sleeve behind the wrist is no longer horizontal. The area above the white glove worn by Mrs. Kennedy contains the detail of the clothing worn by the spectators in the background where in photo (A), it cannot be seen.

Other inconsistencies exist. The finely distinguished hairline on the president's head, as well as the clarity and size of his head, is visible in photo (B), and a black streak extending from his shoulder to the right above the seat cannot be seen in the first version. In the first version, the president's head appears much smaller. Also in photo (B) the outline of the president's shoulder is visible, where in the first version, this area remains gray in texture.

The motorcycle police officer can be seen next to the car in both photos, yet when the Altgens photo is compared to Frame 255 of the Zapruder film, Commission Exhibit #901 (the frame which the Commission concluded corresponded to the Altgens photograph), it is simply just not there! If the photo truly corresponds to Frame 255, why is it that we cannot see the motorcycle next to the president's car in Commission Exhibit #901?

The differences when comparing the two photos raise serious questions and puzzling doubts. Why are the photos different? Was the first version touched? Could this one photo be the key to resolving why the FBI entered the New York Associated Press office on the morning of 23 November, 1963 and subsequently confiscated all the photos which were taken in Dealey Plaza? Why would the FBI be concerned about the photos? Was it hiding something?

Photograph from Zapruder Film   *Photograph from Reenactment*

DISTANCE TO STATION C .... 181.9 FT.

DISTANCE TO RIFLE IN WINDOW .... 218.0 FT.

ANGLE TO RIFLE IN WINDOW .... 18°03'

DISTANCE TO OVERPASS .... 307.1 FT.

ANGLE TO OVERPASS .... 0°44'

Photograph through Rifle Scope   *Frame 255*

Commission Exhibit #901

Commission Exhibit #901 offers both the reenactment of Frame 255 and a still copy of the actual frame. If the Commission's conclusion of the Altgens photo corressponding to Frame 255 were correct, why is it we do not see the motorcycle beside the president's car? Note the reenactment car has gone far beyond the corresponding street stripe adjacent to the car. In order to determine a corresponding frame of the Zapruder film by using the street stripe as a guide, the front tire of the reenactment car must be placed on the stripe. The street stripe behind the reenactment car is that of Frame 210. (Photo courtesy of Assassination Archives and Research Center.)

Author's Note

When I first noted the differences in these photos, I contacted Wide World Photo to question it on why one would have shown clarity, (B), while the other contained very little detail, (A). During this brief discussion, I asked if any changes were made to the photo or if it was washed to add clarity. I was assured that if the changes I pointed out were if fact visible (since it had not seen the photo which appeared in the *New York Daily News*), that it could be a result of a loss suffered while the photo was being sent on the wire and I was assured that the Associated Press did not touch the photo in any way. I noted that the loss suffered in the first version was limited only to the windshield portion of the limousine.

Without examination of the uncropped version, one could conclude that no alteration exists and the difference between the first and second versions was intended by editors working for the newspaper. The basis for a determination such as this would be simply in that the first version was "washed" in order to provide the reader with an enhanced view of the limousine's interior. Washing a photograph gives far greater clarity to the point trying to be made and allows the viewer to quickly see what is taking place without having to study the picture or distinguish between subjects. Thus we could conclude that the first version which appeared in newspapers across the country, was a copy of the original and was "washed" to add clarity.

As our conversation about my interest in the Altgens photograph continued, my source stated, "They....came in and took everything we had related to the assassination!" Who "they" were I can only guess (as I could not get my source to elaborate) was the FBI, as the CIA had no part in the investigation and the Commission had not been created at that time. These people, according to my source, confiscated all the photos in the possession of the Associated Press and my source further stated, "not all these materials were returned."

The Helping Hands Photo

In the third and final version of the Altgens photo further inconsistencies provide us with a far easier concept to conclude that alterations were made to this photo. In the uncropped version of the Altgens photo (the one Senator Yarborough submitted), two men appear in the right-hand margin of the photo. Close examination of these two men shows that they are approximately thirty-five feet apart. The shadow of the man wearing the white coveralls is in direct line with the motorcycle riding to the left rear of the presidential limousine and he is not too far from the tree shadow, which is even with the vice-presidential limousine (third car back).

The man clapping his hands, Charles Brehm, is almost directly across from the fourth street stripe on Elm Street. The size of his hands is consistent with being relatively close to the motorcade and he remains in the horizontal plane of the photo.

When we compare the position of the man in the white coveralls with what the Warren Commission concluded was corresponding Frame 255 (See Commission Exhibit #901), this man can not be found. So not only has the motorcycle not appeared next to the car, this man as well can not be seen. These inconsistencies are proof that the Commission was wrong about Frame 255 corresponding to the Altgens photo. But do they mean it was altered? Why would the interior view of the limousine appear to correspond to Frame 255 while other elements of the photo do not?

The Uncropped Version of the Altgens Photo

The third and final version of the Altgens photo provides the exact location of the Presidential limousine on Elm Street whereby a corresponding frame of the Zapruder film can be determined. According to the FBI, a street stripe is hidden in this photograph by the Secret Service follow-up car, but note the front tire of the presidential limousine has gone slightly beyond the next stripe in the photo. If a stripe is hidden by the car, the photo should correspond to Frame 243, however if there is no stripe, the photo would correspond to Frame 210 or two stripes beyond the tree shadow, forty-five frames before Mrs. Kennedy places her hand on the president's forearm. Also, the Stemmons Freeway sign is directly across from the second street stripe beyond the tree shadow in the Zapruder film, yet no sign appears in this photo! (Photograph courtesy of AP/Wide World Photo.)

39

If Not 255, What Frame?

Commission Exhibit #900, the FBI reenactment photo, provides us with proof that at least the FBI knew the location of the president's car when Altgens took this picture. Would this have escaped the attention of the Warren Commission as well? When we examine the Altgens photo under the pretense of it corresponding to Frame 249 of the Zapruder film, inconsistencies also emerge. Though the motorcycle riding left rear of the president's car appears to be even with the man in the white coveralls, as it does in the Altgens photo, this frame too cannot be the corresponding frame.

If Frame 249 were to be the corresponding frame, based primarily on the shadow of the man in the white coveralls being even with the motorcycle, as it appears that way in the uncropped version of the photo, Secret Service Agent Roy Kellerman seated in front of the Texas governor would be facing to his left center, but he is not. (Notice in all three versions of the Altgens photo just how far Agent Kellerman is facing to his left.) In fact this Secret Service agent will not be facing around to the left center as he appears in the Altgens photo until Frame 255, at a point far beyond where the shadow of the man in the white coveralls becomes even with the motorcycle.

Notice Agent Kellerman is looking far to his right in Commission Exhibit #899 and also keep in mind that the direction of the sun would have prevented the shadow of the man in the white coveralls from lining up at any given point after Frame 249 of the film. Since the motorcade was moving at approximately twelve miles per hour, this is the only possible frame of the film where we find the man in the white coveralls in this position! Troubled?

What about Charles Brehm?

Brehm, who should be seen within the next few frames in order for his shadow to be across from the fourth street stripe on Elm Street (See Commission Exhibit #901) will not appear until Frame 273, which is nearly thirty-five feet further down Elm Street or two more street stripes. Puzzling?

What this means is that by Frame 249, the shadow of the man in the white coveralls lines up with the motorcycle, thus making Frame 249 the corresponding frame to the Altgens photo *with one exception*. Roy Kellerman is *not* facing forward and won't be until Frame 255, at a point in time when both the motorcycle is missing and the shadow of the man in the white coveralls no longer lines up with the motorcycle riding left rear of the presidential limousine. But let's not forget Charles Brehm. In the uncropped version of the Altgens photo, it appears that he is relatively close to the street stripe which the president's car has reached. Yet in the Zapruder film, the car will need to pass a minimum of one stripe after Frame 255 to reach the location in which Brehm was actually standing.

Photograph from Zapruder Film

Photograph from Reenactment

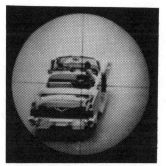

Photograph through Rifle Scope

DISTANCE TO STATION C .... 175.5 FT.

DISTANCE TO RIFLE IN WINDOW .... 211.9 FT.

ANGLE TO RIFLE IN WINDOW .... 18°32'

DISTANCE TO OVERPASS .... 313.1 FT.

ANGLE TO OVERPASS .... 0°48'

Frame 249

Commission Exhibit #899

The president's car, now well beyond Frame 210, hasn't quite reached Frame 255. Note the location of the man in the white coveralls to the left rear of the motorcade. The motorcade did not stop, but continued on through Dealey Plaza as the shots rang out. If we were to conclude that the Altgens photo corresponded to any frame after this point, the man in the white coveralls would no longer line up with the motorcycle. (See uncropped version.) If this were the corresponding frame, we would see Agent Roy Kellerman facing left center. (Photo courtesy of Assassination Archives and Research Center.)

Think about it! The Altgens photo should correspond to the frame in which the shadow of the man in the white coveralls lines up with the motorcycle riding left rear, but what we see in the windshield portion of the Altgens photo is different compared to what we see happening in the presidential limousine.

Puzzling at Best—Let's Try the Tree Shadow

If the Altgens photo was a genuine, untouched, unaltered photograph taken on the day of the assassination, we could expect that the tree shadow which appears in the uncropped version, to be consistent with a comparative frame of the Zapruder film. In comparison to the Zapruder film, however, as the vice presidential limousine rounds the corner from Houston Street onto Elm Street, the president's car passes the tree shadow and continues to the exact position it was in when Altgens took his photo. (See uncropped version.) The Elm Street road stripes can be counted in both the Zapruder film and the Altgens photo.

One stripe.

Another stripe.

The tree shadow.

Another stripe.

Then the president's car reaches the *second* street stripe west of the tree shadow. By calculating the exact location of the vice presidential limousine as being even with the tree shadow, as it appears in the Altgens photo, this would put the president's car at Frame 210, or forty-five frames before Frame 255, not after as the Commission has suggested. The Warren Commission concluded that Frame 255 of the Zapruder film compared to the Altgens photo when in fact it appears that Frame 210 would be a better guess. With the exception of what appears to be happening inside the limousine, the freeway sign not seen in the Altgens photo in comparison to the street stripes, and the location of the man in the hard hat, Frame 210 is without question the corresponding frame!

Diagram 6

Locations of presidential limousine on street stripes

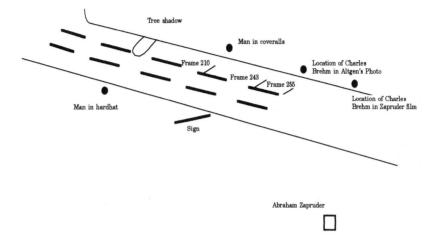

Note: When examining the uncropped version, count the street stripes down Elm Street from the tree shadow. The president's car must be placed on the second one if the tree shadow and the stripes are to be used as a guide for determining the location of the limousine when Altgens snapped his picture.

Professional Warlocks

Listening to the Warren Commission report the findings of the Altgens photo and the rhetoric such a study portrays seems to convey the message that the Commission knew there was a conspiracy and that the Altgens photo was altered.

The Report states, "Another photographer, Philip L. Willis, snapped a picture at a time *which he also asserts was simultaneous with the first shot.* Analysis of his photograph revealed that it was taken at approximately *Frame 210* of the Zapruder film, which was the approximate time of the shot that probably hit the President and the Governor. If Willis accurately recalled that there were no previous shots, this would be strong evidence that the first shot did not miss."

Once again confusion abounds as the Commission concluded that the Willis photo corresponded to Frame 210 and that it was taken as a result of hearing the sound of the first shot. In the Willis photo, the president has not yet reacted to the first bullet strike, so why would the Commission have concluded that the president was shot behind the sign? Remember both the Altgens photo and the Willis photo were taken as a result of hearing what they both felt was the first shot, but we see no sign of the president reacting to a bullet strike in the Willis photo.

In the Willis photo, notice that the Secret Service follow-up car and the motorcycle riding adjacent to it have just slightly passed the first street stripe beyond the tree shadow. Secret Service Agents Clint Hill and Bill McIntyre are next to the stripe. Notice that President Kennedy, who appears to be looking slightly to his right, shows no sign of being struck at this point in time.

The uncropped version of the Altgens photo shows the distance between the Secret Service follow-up car and the presidential limousine to be minimal. These similarities can be found also in the Willis photo. Also, a man in a hard hat can be seen in the right-hand margin of the Willis photo and can be viewed next to the lamppost in the Altgens photograph. In comparison to the Zapruder film, the Willis photo has corresponding similarities at about Frame 200, based primarily on the location of the Secret Service car to the tree shadow.

Grassy Knoll
above and to right
of motorcade

Bill Newman
with his wife and
two children

Freeway sign

Abraham Zapruder

Man in
hard hat

Willis Photo

Above is the Phil Willis photo the Warren Commission corresponded to Frame 210 of the Zapruder film. Note the proximity of the street stripe next to the Secret Service car which has gone slightly by the tree shadow. Note also the man in the hard hat in the right-hand margin of the photo. From this photo is doesn't appear that there could have been a stripe hidden by the Secret Service follow-up car in the Altgens photo. (Photo courtesy of Phil Willis–Copyright to 2039.)

Frame 210—Cover-up Deception of Commission Exhibit #893

Another method of determining which frame of the Zapruder film corresponded to the Altgens photo would be to locate the frame in which the two Secret Service agents riding on the right-side running boards are looking back towards the Depository. If it were possible to locate these men looking backwards, our task would be an easy one.

Frame 210 of the Zapruder film has not been released to the public for thirty years! Why? The Warren Commission had Frame 210 in its possession as it appeared in the Official Report in Commission Exhibit #893. In the Altgens photo, notice that the two Secret Service agents riding the passenger-side running boards of the presidential limousine are looking back towards the Depository. If the Altgens photo truly corresponds to Frame 210 when we examine it, would we see the two Secret Service agents looking back at the Depository? Why did the Commission crop Frame 210? Why did the Commission cut it out of the film and not publish these frames in its report? It had indicated that the Willis photo corresponded to Frame 210, but provided no evidence to substantiate this claim.

In Volume 18 of the twenty-six-volume set of books printed by the Warren Commission, the complete Zapruder film can be found printed in black and white frames, but complete is not a good word to use. Frames 208, 209, 210, and 211 were cut from the film and were not printed in Volume 18 of the report. We know that Frame 210 was examined by the Commission and the FBI and that we can view a cropped version in the Official Report along with the reenactment photo taken by the FBI. But why has it been cropped? (See Commission Exhibit #893.)

As with any eight millimeter camera, the film utilizes two sprocket holes as guides for the film as it is being run through the camera. The guides are cut out of the film when produced, but this does not limit the camera's ability to use the portion of the film between the guides. Motion pictures use the entire width of the film when they are being taken. Therefore when producing still photographs during photo process editing from eight millimeter film, professionals in this field often crop the sprocket holes from the film for a better-looking picture. To this day, any version of the Zapruder film shown by the media on television has been cut or cropped. The films used by CBS, NBC, and other affiliate and non-affiliate stations will be found to *not* have these frames included in their copies.

When examining Frames 207 and 212 in the Official Report, both show the two Secret Service agents in the sprocket margins of the film, but we were not allowed to view them in Frames 208 through 211 because the Commission did not place them into exhibit.

Photograph from Zapruder Film

Photograph from Reenactment

Photograph through Rifle Scope

DISTANCE TO STATION C .... 138.9 FT.

DISTANCE TO RIFLE IN WINDOW .... 176.9 FT.

ANGLE TO RIFLE IN WINDOW .... 21°34'

DISTANCE TO OVERPASS .... 348.8 FT.

ANGLE TO OVERPASS .... +0°22'

Frame 210

Commission Exhibit #893

Why was Frame 210 of the Zapruder film cropped? Note the tire of the presidential limousine has reached a street stripe at Frame 210. No stripes were hidden by the Stemmons Freeway sign and the president's car will reach the next stripe at Frame 243. (Photo courtesy of Assassination Archives and Research Center.)

The only version of Frame 210 that has been printed and released to the public has been cropped, making it impossible to determine if these two men are indeed looking back at the Depository. It is likely that if Agents Landis and Ready can be seen in Frames 207 and 212, they are sure to appear in Frames 208 through 211. It is clear that either the Warren Commission or the FBI is concealing whatever these four frames have to offer, but do we need these frames to conclude that the Altgens photo was altered? Does it correspond to Frame 210?

The Street Stripes

The detail of the painted street stripes which appear in the uncropped version, the location of the motorcade, and the background scene in relation to these stripes, should provide us with concise measurements to determine the location of the presidential limousine when Altgens took this photo and then allow us to select a corresponding frame of the Zapruder film. By reviewing the Zapruder film, it is clear that as the Secret Service car and the vice-presidential car proceed to the corresponding locations in the Altgens photo, the presidential limousine reaches the white painted street mark with its front tire at Frame 210.

In freeze-frame viewing with a video cassette recorder or by still photographs of the Zapruder film, the men who appear in the right-hand margin of the uncropped version simply do not appear in the Zapruder film when the president's car reaches this position (Commission Exhibit #893). The man in the white coveralls cannot be seen in Frame 210. However the motorcycle to the left rear of the presidential limousine is in consistent location to correspond with the Altgens photo if it is behind the sign.

There are only four street stripes from the corner of Houston Street to what Frame 210 represents in the Zapruder film. The fourth stripe can be seen in the Zapruder film just as the Presidential limousine emerges from behind the Stemmons Freeway sign. If there were no other stripes on Elm Street, Frame 210 is without question the corresponding frame of the Altgens photo.

A Review of the Facts

1. Frame 255 of the Zapruder film in a still-photo copy does not show the motorcycle next to the passenger door in front of Governor Connally. It is clear in all three versions of the Altgens photo that the motorcycle is *very close* to the car and the officer appears to be looking at the president. The man in the white coveralls is also missing.

2. The FBI re-enacted Frame 255 of the Zapruder film and reported to the Commission. Neither the Commission nor the FBI provided the detail of the missing motorcycle or the man in the white coveralls when they concluded that Frame 255 corresponded to the Altgens photo and it is unclear how they could have missed missing the motorcycle, the man in the white coveralls, or the man clapping his hands. Instead the Commission chose to conclude that the Altgens photo corresponded to Frame 255 and provide us only with a cropped version of this photo; so we would not be able to tell the difference. Also, the FBI re-enactment shows the president's car far beyond the fifth street stripe. Therefore because of these inconsistencies, we can conclude, beyond a reasonable doubt, that Frame 255 is not the corresponding frame.

3. Commission Exhibit #893 (showing Frame 210) displaces the two men in the right-hand margin of the Altgens photo as well, and the motorcycle officer, although he cannot be seen, could be behind the Stemmons Freeway sign. Other than placing another reenactment car on the street stripe (which is no longer there) and taking a photo from where Abraham Zapruder was standing, we would need to view the uncropped missing frames of the Zapruder film in order to determine if in fact Agents Landis and Ready were indeed looking back at the Depository.

4. Knowing that a sloppy job was done on photo (A) and that photo (B) contained even more detail, we cannot dismiss the account that Mrs. Kennedy's hand does not reach the president's forearm until Frame 255, regardless of the position of the motorcade at Frame 210 of the Zapruder film or the corresponding Altgens photo.

5. The FBI provided the Commission with incomplete information regarding the Altgens photo, but it is on record and recorded in the exhibits of the Commission with Yarborough's uncropped version. It is fair to assume that the Warren Commission and the FBI officially knew about the photo alterations, but if they did not (and it is my opinion they did), the framing of the evidence to alter photos provides a clear option to the plausible front entry wounds sustained by President Kennedy.

It now may be understandable why the Warren Commission published only the cropped version of the Altgens photo. (See aerial photo of Dealey Plaza.) By estimating the location of the president's car in reference to the stone pillar and the close proximity of the crowd in the background to the motorcade, we can calculate the approximate location of the president's car when Altgens took his photograph. We can then view the corresponding frame by placing the president's car in about the same area while viewing the Zapruder film. If the photo alterations did not include the street stripes (which in my opinion are in their genuine location), Frame 210 corresponds to the Altgens photo and a cover-up conspiracy did in fact take place!

It is my opinion that the Warren Commission and the FBI knew that the Altgens photo was altered, perhaps by methods they were accustomed to using or knew were methods used by central intelligence agencies throughout the world. The Commission could not breach a national security secret and if it had revealed that the photo was altered, it would have also had to admit that Oswald could not have acted alone and there was a conspiracy. The Commission and the FBI hid the truth by not revealing the corresponding frame of the Zapruder film and by not publishing the uncropped version of this photo.

To complete Chapter Two, "A Prologue of Suspicion," I'll conclude that the Warren Commission knew more than what it was telling regarding the Altgens photo and its relation to both the Willis photo and the Zapruder film. The photo alterations can be seen primarily in the windshield portion of the limousine, the motorcycle next to the passenger car door, as well as the two men in the right-hand margin of the uncropped version who were imposed onto a base negative. (See how many alterations you can list.) These likenesses were superimposed on the negative prior to releasing the uncropped version to the public and were taken from subsequent and previous snapshots of the assassination. The windshield portion of the limousine is Frame 255 but the president's car is at Frame 210.

These alterations were not performed by the Associated Press or James Altgens and they can be exonerated of any handling of this photo. It is my opinion, too, that the photo alterations were handled in Dallas. Prior to the release of the photographs, the Associated Press office in New York was visited by FBI officials, who confiscated all the photographs in its possession. What happened to these photos happened while they were in the possession of the FBI, not the Associated Press.

The conspirators needed to buy time in order to destroy any evidence which would prove incriminating. They needed to convince the American public that the shots were fired from behind the motorcade and provided the scene with a diversion which would draw the attention of the Secret Service agents. They were concerned about the public finding out about the conspiracy to kill our president, not the government. These people who orchestrated the assassination had power, power behind them to cover it up and power to convince thousands of people that Oswald acted alone. The photo is deceiving because it is meant to be.

Of course from the information we have examined here although it may be incriminating, one cannot examine this photo with a careful eye and believe after viewing the Zapruder film that the limousine has gone far beyond the Stemmons Freeway sign. The closeness of the motorcade to the tree shadow, the nearby Depository, and the street corner somehow evade the concept that the presidential limousine is such a great distance from the people on the sidewalk. If the Warren Commission's conclusions are right, the presidential limousine in the Altgens photograph is eighty-seven feet from the tip of the third street stripe on Elm Street near the tree shadow. (See uncropped version.) According to the Zapruder film, the fourth street stripe on Elm Street places the presidential limousine at Frame 210 or forty-five feet from this point.

In the Altgens photo, we see only four stripes, so why the big mix-up? How long are the street stripes? What is the distance between each stripe? Does the distance vary or does it remain the same?

The FBI reenactment photo (Commission Exhibit #900) indicates that a street stripe was hidden by the Secret Service car trailing the presidential limousine. However this one *fact* doesn't change this chapter—it began it! Was the limousine at Frame 210? Mathematically there could not have been a street stripe hidden behind the Stemmons Freeway sign or under the Secret Service follow-up car which would have gone undetected by the Zapruder film, yet a stripe appears in the reenactment photo. The very next stripe would correspond to the Zapruder film with the presidential limousine at Frame 243 where we can clearly see what is happening as a result of a second shot fired in Dealey Plaza.

Roy Kellerman looking far to the right, no motorcycle next to the car, the man in the white coveralls nowhere near the motorcycle, and Mrs. Kennedy's hand nowhere near the president. If the FBI reenactment photo is genuine, the car would be on the fifth street stripe on Elm Street, or Frame 243!

Many eyewitness accounts suggested that the shots did not come from the Depository, even though on the day after the assassination, this photo convinced many people that they had!

Frame 243—Kellerman Car on Street Stripe

Frame 243 places the presidential limousine on the fifth street stripe on Elm Street. Notice Agent Kellerman seated in front of John Connally, facing far to his right. If the street stripes in the FBI reenactment photo are genuine, this frame if proof that the Altgens photo was altered to produce the effects of the shots coming from the Depository. Also note that Mrs. Kennedy's hand is nowhere near the president's forearm and could not have been seen through the windshield portion of the Altgens photograph.

Dealey Plaza—Scene of Assassination
Aerial view. Dallas, Texas. (Photograph courtesy of Assassination Archives and Research Center.)

Chapter Three

The Three Faces of Lee

Lee Harvey Oswald, the lone gunman reported to have shot President John F. Kennedy from the sixth floor window of the Texas School Book Depository, did not admit to this allegation. When asked by news reporters in the halls of the Dallas police station and when later asked by yet another reporter if he had shot the president, Oswald stated that law enforcement officials had not asked him that question. Oswald did not deny having knowledge of the assassination but did imply by his statement that he was a suspect but had not been charged with the president's death at that time.

The Commission investigated the possibility of a conspiracy taking place, but the execution of the investigation can be regarded as inadequate. At the onset of looking into a possible conspiracy, the Commission *"faced substantial difficulties."*

The Report continues, "Prior to his own death Oswald had neither admitted his own involvement nor implicated any other person in the assassination of President Kennedy."

Lee Harvey Oswald's guilt had been established by an entire chapter which the Commission devoted to "Investigation of Possible Conspiracy." This began the biography of Oswald with his relationship to Jack Ruby, while the physical evidence provided the Commission with presumably no insight and was dismissed and filed with the "negatives."

Was there a lone assassin? Oswald issued this statement to scores of news reporters at the Dallas police station.

"I really don't know what the situation is about, nobody has told me anything except that I have been accused of ah, of murdering a policeman. I know nothing more than that, I do request someone to come forward and to give me a legal assistance."

When asked, "Did you kill the president?" Oswald replied, "No. I have not been charged with that. In fact nobody has said that to me yet. The

54

first thing I heard about it; was when the news people that reported it in the hall, asked me that question."

Lee Harvey Oswald's innocence relied heavily upon his own statement made to the press just hours after his arrest. He was subsequently charged with the murders of President Kennedy and Officer J.D. Tippit. Oswald's arrest and interrupted transfer to the county jail was witnessed by reporters and newsmen at the Dallas police station, where many photographs and recorded interviews were taken. Not only did Oswald's statement to the reporters indicate that he was innocent of shooting the president, but he was also being denied legal council and the clothing he was wearing and his alibi remained consistent with eyewitness accounts.

Oswald's guilt was based primarily on evidence presented to the Commission by the Dallas police department. It was reported that Oswald carried a package into the Texas School Book Depository on the morning of the assassination by a witness who drove Oswald to work that morning. Oswald reportedly told him they were curtain rods. Oswald denied this claim and stated he never spoke to this man about curtain rods. This witness never saw a rifle and reported that the article was concealed in a brown paper bag.

Blind Man's Bluff

Where was Oswald when the president was assassinated? Was he the lone gunman or did Oswald give repeated testimony to Dallas police officials, the Secret Service, and the FBI as to his whereabouts? Can it be substantiated by Oswald's testimony that he could not have been on the sixth floor of the Texas School Book Depository at the time the shots rang out? Is there more than one photograph that places Oswald in a different location as the motorcade passed the Depository building?

The information needed to answer these questions was examined by the Warren Commission and as you will learn, this evidence was not considered to be credible. It is impossible to be in two places at one time and there is photographic evidence of Oswald's location while the assassination was being carried out. Was Oswald on the sixth floor? is a question you must answer. The facts are available now as they were thirty years ago.

It was reported by the Commission that the man standing in the doorway of the Depository building at the time the motorcade passed was Billy Nolan Lovelady, a Book Depository worker.

The Report reads, "The man on the front steps of the building, thought or alleged by some to be Lee Harvey Oswald, is actually Billy Lovelady, an employee of the Texas School Book Depository, who somewhat resembles Oswald."

Lovelady testified to being the man in the Altgens photo and does resemble Oswald; in fact their similarity to one another is disturbing. However, the man seen in the Depository doorway does resemble Oswald, because it is Oswald. According to research conducted by Josiah Thompson, author of *Six Seconds in Dallas*, the FBI reported that Lovelady was wearing a red and white striped, short-sleeve shirt the day of the assassination. But when CBS picked up on the shirt discrepancies, Lovelady stated that he was wearing a different shirt when questioned and photographed by the FBI. I find it hard to believe that J. Edgar Hoover's FBI would document Lovelady's official statement and allow the president's Commission to conclude that the man in the doorway was Lovelady and not Oswald.

The Commission concluded otherwise, but are there facts and were there other photographs taken while the motorcade moved slowly by the Depository which can relate to the man being Oswald? Certainly, if the man in the Altgens photo was Oswald, there could be no discrepancy as to Oswald being on the sixth floor of the Depository at the time the motorcade passed by the building. What is the man in the photo wearing and what was Oswald wearing when he was arrested? If the Commission's account is the truth, then both Lovelady and Oswald wore the same clothes on 22 November, 1963.

The Interrogation of Oswald

There is conclusive evidence that Oswald, after leaving the Depository that afternoon, went directly to the theater where he was subsequently arrested and charged with the shooting of Dallas police officer, J.D. Tippit. According to the Warren Commission, however, Oswald returned first to his boarding house and then proceeded to the theater. Inspector Thomas Kelly of the Secret Service interrogated Oswald in Dallas a short time after the assassination of the president and filed this report.

> In response to questions put by Captain Fritz, Oswald said that *immediately after having left the building where he worked, he went by bus to the theater;* where he was arrested; that when he got on the bus he secured a transfer and thereafter transferred to other buses to get to his destination. He denied that he brought a package to work on that day and he denied that he had ever had any conversation about curtain rods with the boy named Wesley who drove him to his employment.

A contradiction which can be linked only to the reports of other officers who questioned Oswald regarding the clothing he was wearing and his route to the theater raises serious doubt concerning the validity of the reports. If Inspector Kelly's account of Oswald saying he went immediately to the theater is correct, can we find other evidence to support Inspector Kelly's account of Oswald's claims as opposed to those of the FBI?

The reports filed by James P. Hosty and James W. Bookhout can be questioned, as these reports indicate that Oswald said he went home to change his clothes prior to going to the theater, because they were dirty.

One report reads, "After hearing what had happened, he (Oswald) said that because of all the confusion there would be no work performed that afternoon so he decided to go home. Oswald stated he *went home by bus and changed his clothes and went to a movie.*"

A separate report filed by James Bookhout reads, "After arriving at his apartment, he changed his shirt and trousers because they were dirty. He described his dirty clothes as being a *reddish colored, long sleeve,* shirt with a button down collar and gray colored trousers. He indicated that he had placed these articles of clothing in the lower drawer of his dresser."

The shirt Oswald reportedly changed out of was red with long sleeves, but Inspector Kelly reported that Oswald stated that he went immediately to the theater, indicating that he didn't change. What these reports lead us to believe is that Oswald had not only changed his clothes, but he had changed his story about the route he took when he left the Depository.

The Commission's report indicates that "Oswald's shirt, which he was wearing at the time of the arrest, had been removed and sent to the crime lab in Washington with all the other evidence for a comparison test. Oswald said he would like to have a shirt from his clothing that had been brought to the office to wear over the T-shirt that he was wearing at the time."

Oswald was furious when the Washington authorities removed his shirt and demanded to know where it was and why it had been taken from him, but from reading the official version, one can visibly see how cooperative Oswald was being with the investigators.

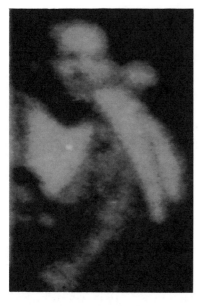

Suspected Assassin Oswald

Suspected assassin Lee Harvey Oswald told newsman and reporters repeatedly that he was a "patsy." The photo above shows the man in the doorway of the Texas School Book Depository as the motorcade passed by. Is it possible to be in two places at one time?

The Warren Commission concluded that this man was Billy Lovelady, a man who resembled Oswald. What are the chances of Lovelady not only looking like Oswald, but also dressing like him?

(Top two photos courtesy of AP/Wide World Photo, bottom photo courtesy of Jim Murray, Life Magazine, © Time Warner Inc.)

Did Oswald Change His Clothing?

By Oswald's statement to Inspector Kelly, we learned that he went straight to the theater. He did not go home and change his clothing, but was asked to remove his shirt and changed at the police station. The possibility exists that Oswald wasn't being truthful with the inspector, however the clothing worn by Oswald at the time of his arrest has striking resemblance to the clothing worn by the man in the Depository doorway as seen in the Altgens photo. The shirt Oswald was wearing when he was arrested resembles both the texture and the style of dress seen worn by the man in the Altgens photograph standing in the doorway of the Depository.

If the photos compare and it is substantial evidence that Oswald was indeed wearing the exact style and type of shirt worn when he was arrested compared to the man in the doorway, it is conclusive proof that Oswald very well may be that man. The shirt worn by the man in the doorway was a long-sleeved, heavy, textured shirt which was unbuttoned down to about the first button above the waistline. It provided the exposure of the white T-shirt in the shape of a large "V." The T-shirt resembles a crew neck and the face of the man resembles Oswald. The receding hairline is visible as the sunlight shines on his face. The shirt is worn with the sleeves rolled down.

When Oswald was arrested, the shirt he had on resembled the shirt worn by the man in the doorway in all aspects. The sleeves are rolled down. The shirt is unbuttoned to the waistline which exposes his T-shirt in the shape of a large "V." Too, Oswald's receding hairline seen in photo after his arrest bears striking resemblance to the receding hairline of the man in the doorway. The shirt seen in the photo taken a short time after Oswald's arrest was subsequently removed and sent to the FBI crime laboratory in Washington, but does not compare to the color of the shirt worn by the man in the doorway. The man in the doorway had on a red shirt while the shirt sent to Washington was light brown.

With the fact that Oswald indicated by his statement to Inspector Kelly that (he) went straight to the theater after leaving the Depository, along with the photographic evidence showing Oswald's clothing at the time of his arrest being the same as those worn by the man in the doorway, it is my opinion that Oswald could not have shot President Kennedy and was the man in the doorway. From a brief analysis of the photos, it is difficult to conclude that Oswald went home and changed into the same clothes worn by Billy Lovelady.

It is also easy to conclude from the treatment Oswald received at the Dallas police station that he was given other clothes to wear for the purpose of not revealing the fact that the shirt he had on when he was arrested was red. The photographic evidence is conclusive and even if Oswald did go home and change his dirty clothes, the shirt he was wearing while at the Depository was still red. (re: FBI reports)

We've Got the Wrong Man!

The Altgens photo was black and white. Therefore the red shirt Oswald was reported to have taken off when he went home cannot be clarified by the photo, if indeed the man is Oswald. Photographs taken of Oswald at time of his arrest (in front of the theater) indicate that he had on a reddish-colored shirt, but these photographs show only a glimpse of Oswald's shirt as he was being placed into a Dallas police car.

In Chapter Two we discussed how the Altgens photo was altered by using a base negative to create a scene which simply does not correspond to any frame of the Zapruder film. So how can we conclude if Oswald or Lovelady was even there when the motorcade passed the building? As confusing as this may seem, how can a photograph be used to exonerate Oswald of firing the shots in Dallas if the photo was clearly altered? If the photo is not genuine, how can we say that the man standing in the doorway was even there at the time the motorcade turned the corner from Houston Street onto Elm Street?

Robert Hughes, who stood at the south end of Houston Street, filmed the presidential motorcade just as it began its turn onto Elm Street. This film reveals that the man in the doorway at the time the motorcade passed had on a red, long-sleeved shirt, buttoned down to expose the T-shirt in the shape of a "V" and provides further proof that the man in the doorway can only be Oswald and he may have been there all the while the motorcade passed the building. Did Oswald go home and change? Or did Dallas police officials take part in framing Oswald?

Inspector Kelly also filed this report. "....he asked me whether I was an FBI agent and I said that I was not, that I was a member of the Secret Service. He said when he was standing in front of the Textbook Building and about to leave it, a young crew cut man rushed up to him and said he was from the Secret Service, showed a book of identification, and asked him where the phone was. Oswald said he pointed toward the pay phone in the building and that he saw the man actually go to the phone before he left."

The report also indicated that Oswald was handed some different clothing to put on. The clothing included a sweater. (These were articles Oswald had on when he was being transferred to the county jail.)

Man in the Doorway

This frame from an eight millimeter film was taken by Robert Hughes just as the president's car began its descent down Elm Street. In it the man in the doorway of the Depository can be seen wearing a red, long-sleeved shirt with the front buttoned down to expose the T-shirt in the shape of a "v". This photograph is proof that at least the man remained there while Hughes took his photograph. If the man is Oswald, it cannot be verified by this photo, but the shirt is red and does compare once again to the shirt Oswald had on when he was arrested. Also, note that two people can be seen to the left of the sixth floor "assasin's window". The Commission provided no information concerning these people nor did it report what they saw or heard. (Photograph courtesy of Robert Hughes.) (This photograph was unavailable to author at time of printing.)

A similar view of the Depository to the Robert Hughes footage, shown here, was taken by Phil Willis just moments after the assassination. Mr. Willis wrote to me saying, "Oswald may have been the 'patsy,' maybe history will tell? But the head shot from the right front blew his brains up and backwards to the left rear of JFK's Lincoln. For an instant the air above JFK's head was like a red halo—a brilliant flash of color and light. And we knew he was dead." The arrow indicates the location of the man in the doorway in both the Altgens photo and the Robert J. E. Hughes eight millimeter film. I asked Mr. Willis if the sound he heard comng from the depository could have been an echo. He said, "Yes, it very well could have been." (Photograph courtesy of Phil Willis–Copyright to 2039.)

At times in his report, Inspector Kelly indicated that when questioned by other officers, Oswald indicated that he changed his clothing before going to the theater, yet Kelly specifically described his interview with Oswald and reported he immediately went to the theater. The inconsistencies appear in regard to the reports offered by Bookhout and Hosty, whereas the report of Secret Service Agent Thomas Kelly remains consistent to the photographs taken of Oswald in Dealey Plaza, at the Texas theater, and at the Dallas police station. At exactly what point in time Oswald was standing in front of the Depository when the young, crew cut man approached him cannot be determined by the Official Report or the reports filed by the Dallas police. It may have been Bill McIntyre. (See Motorcade and Altgens.)

Was It Lee Harvey Oswald?

It is clear, by examining the photos, that Oswald was probably the man in the doorway. Who then was Billy Nolan Lovelady? And what is his part in this whole event? If Oswald indicated that he was standing in front of the doorway, was he there all along? How much time had passed between the assassination and when the young, crew cut man entered the Depository? What time did Oswald leave the building? What time did the Secret Service arrive at Dealey Plaza, upon leaving Parkland Hospital? The Commission said Oswald left at 12:35, about the time the motorcade reached the hospital.

The photograph taken at the time of Oswald's arrest shows him wearing the same shirt as the man in the Altgens photograph. (Commission Exhibit #900) This photo and others provide conclusive proof to determining where Oswald was when the president was shot. The film taken by Robert Hughes shows the motorcade passing the Depository as well. In it, the man in the doorway of the Depository can be seen wearing a red shirt. However the Commission holds in exhibit Oswald's shirt, not red, but brown. The reports offer contradictions of facts which can only be linked to Oswald saying one thing and changing his story or to the Dallas authorities realizing that they had the wrong man, but doing their best to convince us that Oswald had shot the president. When examined, the photos prove beyond a reasonable doubt that Oswald could not and did not kill President Kennedy and the Warren Commission and the FBI blew the investigation.

The Backyard Photos

The backyard photographs taken of Oswald were credible evidence that tied the 6.5 millimeter Mannlicher-Carcano rifle to the assassination of President Kennedy. These photos became know as Commission Exhibits #133-A, #133-B, and #134 (an enlargement of #133-A). No photographs of Oswald or any other assassin holding this rifle were taken on the day of the assassination. The evidence of the gun in relation to the photograph showing Oswald holding the rifle is circumstantial and proves nothing. The Warren Commission knew this!

Assassination researcher Jack White of Fort Worth, Texas has claimed to have proven beyond any question of a doubt that the backyard photographs taken of Oswald were forgeries. White, who has spent years researching the death of President Kennedy, assisted by Jim Marrs, author of *Crossfire– The Plot That Killed Kennedy*, produced the home video "Who Didn't Kill...JFK." The Warren Commission Report indicates that the authenticity of the backyard photographs had been established by expert testimony, but similar to the way the Altgens photo was altered, the backyard photos too provide conclusive proof that a conspiracy did in fact take place.

Robert Blakey, chief council and member of the House Select Committee on Assassinations stated, "If they are invalid, how they were produced poses far reaching questions in the area of conspiracy; for they invent a high degree of technical satisfaction that would almost necessarily raise the possibility that more than private parties conspired not only to kill the President but to make Oswald a patsy."

This area of the assassination has been addressed completely and concisely in the home video "Who Didn't Kill...JFK."

Photographs of Oswald while in the USSR and while in custody of the Dallas police provided the Commission with comparison photographs to use with the backyard photos. Oswald's recollection of the backyard photos is quite vivid as he regarded them as fake. Oswald, while in custody of the Dallas police, was shown the photographs within hours after his arrest. The photos were presumably found in a garage where Oswald had stored some things.

When the Dallas police showed the photos to Oswald, he sneered at them saying that they were fake photos. Oswald said that he had been photographed a number of times the day before and apparently after they photographed him, they superimposed on the photographs a rifle and put a gun in his pocket. Oswald then became very unruly to the police officials. He reportedly argued with them and refused to answer further questions regarding the photos and said that at a proper time he would show that the photos were fake. Why would Oswald indicate that he had been photographed the day before? Who took the photos? Why were pictures taken of Oswald the day before the president was assassinated?

Commission Exhibit #133-A

Commission Exhibit #133-B

Commission Exhibit #134
(Enlargement of Commission Exhibit #133-A)

Commission Exhibits #133-A and #133-B

Much in the same way the Altgens photograph was produced, this photo shows Oswald with the 6.5 millimeter rifle found in the Depository building. Oswald denied ever seeing these photos and became very unruly when they were shown to him at the Dallas police station. "They are fake!" he shouted, "and I'll prove it." He never got his chance. (Photos courtesy of Assassination Archives and Research Center.)

Oswald never did get a chance to defend himself, but was rushed quickly off to the county jail where in route he was subsequently murdered by Jack Ruby, a Dallas nightclub owner. Ruby's only account of his motive to kill Oswald was to save the widow, Mrs. Kennedy, from a long trial. If Oswald had lived, history would not have been recorded the way it was. Even so, what makes history is truth, not fiction. The evidence and the conspiracy to convict Lee Harvey Oswald began prior to 22 November, 1963. Oswald knew he was a patsy but felt confident that he would be set free. His statement to Thomas Kelly and the press provide the reasonable doubt concerning his innocence, while the photographic evidence is substantial proof that Oswald couldn't have been in two places at one time. Oswald's statement to Investigator Thomas Kelly raises the question as to his presumed guilt, unfair treatment, and twisting of his testimony before he had an opportunity to speak with an attorney.

Perhaps from experience Inspector Kelly knew Oswald was being framed; the reports filed by Kelly indicate that Oswald was looking for a friend in Dallas and that he truly had no one and nowhere to turn.

It is not necessary for a trained eye to look at the Altgens photo and determine who the man in the doorway was or even how the photos were altered. Oswald had indicated in testimony that he was in front of the Depository, yet the Commission concluded he was Billy Lovelady. What does the Commission know that it hasn't told us about Lee Harvey Oswald?

For the purposes of history Lee Harvey Oswald may have been many things to many people. He may have had more than one name, but he was not on the sixth floor of the Textbook building in Dallas when the president was shot. The facts about Oswald's participation in the event are contained in the Official Report given to President Johnson and this report contains only information which contradicts Oswald's alibi and can only add to establishing his innocence. If Oswald had any part in the assassination, it is yet to be proven. Though the thickness of the Report suggests a preponderance of evidence against Oswald, the facts we haven't examined disclose the other side of the story.

Everything the Warren Commission reported concerning the assassination of President Kennedy takes us away from Dealey Plaza. Oswald's trip to Russia, his ties to Cuba, his trip through Dallas where J.D. Tippit was killed, his flight to the theater, and the sixth floor window. At a point above and behind the motorcade traveling west on Elm Street. Oswald is dead. The nation has mourned the death of a president and the official versions of the investigation has concluded that Lee Harvey Oswald acted alone. If the information gathered by the researchers of the assassination has provided conclusive determination that the assassination was a cleverly devised conspiracy, what is the evidence? Is there sufficient proof to substantiate these claims? Have researchers adequately investigated all the facts before making their conclusions? How does the work of the researchers compare to the official version? Did the Warren Commission know more than what it was willing to say? Did Lee Harvey Oswald act alone? Was he the patsy he said he was?

As parents of children, most of us have learned that when a child is being picked on for no reason, we can quite readily ascertain why and who's doing the picking. Every child at one time or another displays facial expressions and voices of disapproval for punishment in lieu of a guilty party going free. Lee Harvey Oswald was no different. If we are to accept the fact that Oswald acted alone and that he was not the man in the doorway, then we must conclude right now that all three shots were fired from above and behind the president by Oswald and the other evidence we have yet to examine backed by credible testimony has been prefabricated, or simply misrepresented.

Mirror of Doubt will not ask you to see what can't be seen, judge what cannot be judged, or even hear what cannot be heard. It will just ask that you decide without a reasonable doubt who killed your president. If it wasn't Lee Harvey Oswald, let's move on to a closer look into the mystery surrounding the death of our president, John F. Kennedy.

Chapter Four

Mister X—The Lone Gunman

The epic conclusion of the "grassy knoll assassin theory" is among the most commonly looked at possibilities for determining the location of a second gunman. If the "grassy knoll assassin theory" had been secured during the House Select Committee meetings in the late 1970s, a full scale investigation would have begun. Though the theory posed possibilities, it was nevertheless regarded as being inconclusive based upon the lack of credible evidence that would have linked an assassin to that area. If the theory was indeed correct, any evidence of a gunman firing from that location could not be substantiated from other evidence.

The conclusion of the Commission was, "Based on the evidence analyzed in this chapter (chapter III of the Official Report), the Commission has concluded that the shots which killed President Kennedy and wounded Governor Connally were fired from the sixth floor window at the southeast corner of the Texas School Book Depository Building. *Two bullets probably caused* all the wounds suffered by President Kennedy and Governor Connally. Since the preponderance of the evidence indicated that three shots were fired, the Commission concluded that *one shot probably missed* the Presidential limousine and its occupants, and that the three shots were fired in a time period ranging from approximately 4.8 to an excess of 7 seconds."

The Report also reads, "The three used cartridge cases found near the window on the sixth floor at the southeast corner of the building were fired from the same rifle which fired the above described bullet and fragments, to the exclusion of all other weapons."

The above-described bullet the Commission was referring to was in fact the single bullet found on the stretcher of Governor Connally at Parkland Hospital! It was this bullet that the Warren Commission concluded struck President Kennedy and continued on to hit Governor Connally, yet it was also reported to the Commission by experts that this bullet could not have struck Connally's wrist without sustaining damage.

The Single Bullet Theory

What was the "single bullet theory?" What did it mean? The "single bullet theory," fathered by Chief Council Investigator Arlen Specter, denotes the possibility of a second or even third gunman to have participated in the assassination of President John Kennedy and the subsequent shooting of John Connally. If the Warren Commission's acceptance of the theory was a concise replication of how and when the bullets struck President Kennedy and Texas Governor Connally, we would expect the report to say just that, but it does not. The Warren Commission failed to solve the murder investigation of the president.

The "single bullet" or "stretcher bullet" was fired, according to the Commission, from the sixth floor window and caused the wounds sustained by both the president and the governor, yet its report also indicated that this bullet could not have caused the wrist wounds sustained by Governor Connally. If no other bullets were found and it remained ballistically impossible for the governor's wrist to be damaged by a single bullet, what is the relevancy of this bullet?

The Commission's report also said, "The conclusion that the Governor's wrist was not struck by a pristine bullet (or stretcher bullet) was based on the following."

The report goes into great detail of how the FBI test fired 6.5 millimeter bullets from the rifle found in the Depository into the wrist bone of a cadaver. This conclusion was reached simply because the "stretcher bullet" sustained little damage and could not have caused the wrist wound. Did the bullet cause any wounds? If the governor's wrist was damaged enough where the bullet test fired into the wrist of a cadaver could not substantiate the "stretcher bullet" being found in pristine condition, whose wounds did it cause?

The wrist, in comparison to the other injuries sustained by both men, was most likely to have caused more damage to the bullet after transiting the Governor's back, tearing out a large portion of his fifth rib. The theory is complicated because it cannot by concise calculations, be conclusive evidence to the shots striking both the governor and the president from behind and be backed by expert testimony to verify that the bullet could sustain no damage. There were no other bullets found which could be linked to the president's throat wound and Governor Connally's wounds. The Commission continued to confuse its sixth floor assassin theory with even the most obscure possibilities.

The Report reads, "It is possible that the assassin carried an empty shell in the rifle and fired only two shots, with the witnesses hearing multiple noises made by the same shot. Soon after the three empty cartridges were found, the official at the scene decided that three shots were fired, and that conclusion was widely circulated by the press."

By reading the official version, one can only be confused as to the validity of the information. What did the Commission want you to believe? That three shots were fired? That the assassin carried an empty shell and fired only two? The problem is that the Commission lacked bullets! Of all the fragments found, two were removed from the surface of President Kennedy's brain (which were part of one bullet). Two others were reported by the FBI to have been found in the car and several other fragments were taken from John Connally, but were presumed also to be part of one bullet. There were no other bullets found until the single bullet mysteriously showed up at Parkland Hospital. Yet three shots were fired.

The Dallas Riddle

Governor Connally is the key to understanding the events that transpired in Dallas and brought on the "single bullet theory." Regardless of which shot missed, the Commission concluded that Governor Connally and the president suffered from wounds sustained by a single bullet. In part this was determined from the Parkland Hospital doctors who treated the wounds sustained by the governor and testified that his wounds were caused by one bullet.

The Commission reasoned that "There must be an explanation for Governor Connally's recollection that he was not hit by it." ("It" refers to the bullet that transited the president's windpipe.)

Is there an explanation for the bullet found at Parkland Hospital? It was determined that it did not hit Governor Connally's wrist. The best place for the "stretcher bullet" is where the Commission left it...in the "negative file." The bullet is evidence and can conclusively be added to the cover-up conspiracy in proper perspective.

How was it possible for the Commission to conclude that the "stretcher bullet" did not cause the wrist wound sustained by Governor Connally yet still be fired from the gun found in the Depository to the exclusion of all other weapons?

Kennedys and Connallys in Car
(Photo courtesy of AP/Wide World Photos.)

Refuted Testimony

Governor John B. Connally's recollection of the assassination is one of the most vivid told by the many eyewitnesses on Elm Street the day of the assassination. Governor Connally recalls hearing a rifle shot and said that the shot appeared to have come from over his shoulder. Other eyewitness accounts detail hearing sounds which were similar to firecrackers or motorcycles backfiring coming from just west of the Depository. Yet the Governor knew immediately it was a rifle shot and he thought of nothing else but a rifle shot.

Governor Connally's statement appears in the Official Report submitted to President Johnson. The testimony reads, "We had just made the turn, well, when I heard what I thought was a shot. I heard this noise that I immediately took to be a rifle shot. I instinctively turned to my right because the sound appeared to have come from over my right shoulder, and I saw nothing unusual except just people in the crowd, but I did not catch the President in the corner of my eye, and I was interested because once I heard the shot in my own mind I identified it as a rifle shot and I immediately—the only thought that crossed my mind was that this is an assassination attempt."

If the governor stands correct and he knew it was a rifle shot, having time to turn to the right to try to see the president, it is apparent that an entirely separate bullet struck the president.

The Governor continued, "So I looked, failing to see him...."

This was the official testimony of the Texas governor. However in a nationwide address from his hospital bed, the Texas governor reported somewhat of a puzzling version.

Testifying before the Commission, Connally stated, "I did not catch the president in the corner of my eye...."

The governor continued his recollection before the Commission, "....*failing to see him,* I was turning to look back over my left shoulder into the back seat, but never got that far in my turn. I got about in the position I am facing you, looking a little bit to the left of center, and I felt like someone hit me in the back."

The press immediately picked up on the "single bullet theory" and wanted a response from Governor Connally since his recollection of the event did not provide credibility to the official version. The Commission's reasoning was based primarily on the location of Governor Connally and the president. If the rifle that the Texas governor suggested in testimony was shot from behind, striking only the president, it would have had to hit the governor after it exited the president's throat. This was largely based on a wound found on President Kennedy's body with the trajectory analysis study conducted by the FBI after the autopsy examination in Bethesda.

The "single bullet," "stretcher bullet," or "pristine bullet" (for it has many names) was one possible conclusion, but the Commission concluded this bullet could not have caused the wrist wound of the governor and its conclusion remained contradictory to the doctors at Parkland Hospital. This bullet, which was traveling at a rate faster than 1800 feet per second, could not have just simply plopped out of the president's throat, if it exited his throat. The Commission could not conclude which bullet missed so it didn't conclude which bullet hit! As simple as it seems, the "single bullet theory" was based primarily on the testimony of John Connally.

In response to Arlen Specter, the governor responded to which bullet hit him, by saying, "Well in my judgment it just couldn't have conceivably have been the first one because I heard the sound of the shot. In the first place I don't know anything about the velocity of this particular bullet, but any rifle has a velocity that exceeds the speed of sound, and when I heard the sound of that first shot, that bullet had already reached where I was or it had reached that far, and I heard that shot, I had time to turn to my right, and I started to turn to my left before I felt anything."

Bullets Travel in a Straight Line

It appears from his testimony that Governor Connally not only knew it was a rifle shot from behind, he knew that the shot that struck the president did not hit him. This fact bothered the Warren Commission for the lack of the bullet that struck President Kennedy. We can recall that Dr. Malcolm Perry, the attending physician who treated the president at Parkland Hospital, reported that there appeared to be an entrance wound in the president's throat during his initial examination of the president. Dr. Perry made several attempts to save the president's life which included a tracheostomy incision over the bullet hole.

A 6.5 millimeter bullet (like the one reported to have been fired from the sixth floor) when entering a body would leave a hole approximately the size of the circumference of the bullet. The wound described by Dr. Perry, however, was only three to five millimeters in size or about one-half the size of the wound of entrance created by this type of bullet. Dr. Perry's observations were not exaggerated even though the situation would have bore an extreme amount of pressure. If Dr. Perry was right and the wound noted in the president's throat was an entry wound, we have a possible solution as to why the first bullet did not hit the governor after exiting the president. It came from the front.

The Texas governor was emphatic about his recollection and detailed once again before newsmen and reporters his version of the horrible events in Dallas. Governor Connally said, "I am convinced beyond any question of a doubt. That the first shot did not hit me. Then I was hit. I was not then and I have no memory or recollection of the sound of the shot that hit me. Beyond any question of a doubt, the third shot did not hit me. Unquestionably when the first shot was fired, I recognized it as a shot, I thought of nothing else but it was a rifle shot. I turned to my right, I had time to think, I had time to react, and I turned to my right to look back over my right shoulder to see if I could see anything unusual; particularly to see if I could catch him out of the corner of my eye and I was in the process of turning back to look over my left shoulder. I had come to the point where I was looking straight forward again; when I felt the impact of the bullet that hit me!"

The contradictions of Governor Connally's testimony and the Commission's ruling on the single bullet striking both the president and the governor exist only to where the bullet went after it transited the president's windpipe. Determine where it went and you'll know where it came from. It's that simple. Or at least it should have been!

Contrary to his official testimony to the Warren Commission from Parkland Hospital, Connally reported seeing the president as he turned. He reported that, "I saw the President, he had slumped" but that "he had said nothing." He further stated, "as I turned I was hit." The front entry wound described by Dr. Perry could not be substantiated. However such a bullet entry would contradict both the "single bullet theory" and the testimony of Governor Connally who testified that the shot came from behind. It would also provide further cause for a gunman other than one on the sixth floor of the Depository to indeed be present in the plaza. If Dr. Perry was right, where was the gunman located?

We Have No Way of Telling

The evidence of a front entry wound was ruled out on the basis that no examination of the wound could be performed after the president was pronounced dead. Therefore can we conclude that there aren't adequate grounds to determine if the bullet that struck the president and transited his windpipe came from the front?

Seated in front of the president, the Texas governor, John B. Connally, did not change his official story, but his recollection of the event while at Parkland Hospital did damage the investigation. Connally's testimony to this day is questioned as to the validity, simply on the basis of his recollection of the first bullet not striking him and his reporting seeing the president.

The Commission said that the first bullet may have struck both men and the second could have missed. The third bullet, unless four were fired, hit only the president. I, for one, conclude that Governor Connally was hit by a separate bullet. He was the one who was shot. He would know if anyone knew. If the Zapruder film can substantiate which shot hit the governor, it would also be credible evidence to reflect his entire testimony and the testimony of other eyewitnesses present in Dealey Plaza.

Evidence of Second Gun

From analysis of the Zapruder film, the Commission reported that the president and the governor were behind the sign when the bullet struck both men. As we watch the Zapruder film, however, we see that Governor Connally is facing the car door when it appears that he is struck by the bullet. Careful examination of the film provides concise knowledge of the bullet impacting the governor's back. The bullet that struck Governor Connally was reported medically to have caused all the wounds to his body (back, rib, chest, wrist). As the bullet makes contact with the governor, his face and abdominal motions are indicated by the severe pain associated with a bullet entering a person's body. The reaction of any individual being shot is conclusive, especially if they are being filmed by a movie camera when it occurs.

When the president sustains the damage from the first bullet, his right hand and left hand reach immediately towards his throat. When the third bullet fired in Dealey Plaza impacts the president, his reaction is remarkably visible, as certainly is the location of the gunman.

A close and dear friend spoke to me concerning his reaction to a shot fired at him by a sniper during the war. He recalled feeling a strong blow to his right side and said, "It spun me around in a complete circle." The bullet hit only the web portion of his right hand between the thumb and index finger, yet the velocity of the bullet after striking the stock of the gun whirled him around a complete 180 degrees. This is what one 30 caliber bullet can do to a man and have him walk away. He told me that he had a black and blue mark the size of a softball on his hip for several weeks.

If the reactions of the president being shot are as prevalent as they appear when watching the Zapruder film, are the reactions of Governor Connally conducive to determining which bullet struck him? If for all practical purposes we concur with Connally and disregard the "stretcher bullet," the president would have had to sustain wounds from the first and third bullets from the front and John Connally, the second from behind. This would be consistent with John Connally's version of the event, with one exception!

Tell Us the Truth

Whatever failed the Commission, it wasn't the truth. Governor Connally was telling the truth about the first and third bullets not hitting him and said he did not hear the second shot. Mrs. Connally, seated in front of Mrs. Kennedy to the left of her husband, recalled that she heard a second shot and saw her husband recoil to the right. By concluding that one of the two bullets fired missed Connally, the Commission in effect provided a reasonable escape to the vagueness of its report if it were to determine at a later time which bullet actually struck the governor. It would seem that the testimony would be conducive in promoting research into which bullet hit whom. The trouble with the "single bullet theory" is that it is a work of fiction. It not only could not have happened, it did not happen, and the Commission explains why this is so.

Connally's Wounds Caused By One Bullet

From our reading we recall that the Commission ruled that the "pristine bullet" found on the stretcher occupied by John Connally could not have caused the damage to his wrist. This was the "stretcher bullet."

Now pay close attention. The medical evidence provided credible evidence to suggest that the wounds sustained by Governor Connally were from one bullet.

The report reads, "Ballistic experiments and medical findings establish that the missile which passed through the Governor's wrist and penetrated his thigh had first transversed (passed through) his chest."

When speaking about the "stretcher bullet," the Commission concluded that it was fired from the gun found on the sixth floor. "The three used cartridge cases found near the window on the sixth floor at the southeast corner of the building were fired from the same rifle which fired the above described bullet...."

Now if the "stretcher bullet" did not cause the wounds sustained by the governor, but it was fired from the gun found on the sixth floor and did not hit either the president or the governor, what was the purpose of the "single bullet theory" and why did this nearly whole bullet show up at Parkland Hospital?

Presumably the first bullet should have struck Governor Connally, as the velocity of the bullet exceeded 2000 feet per second. If it were fired from behind as the governor suggested, could it have remained in pristine condition somewhere on his person when he arrived at Parkland Hospital? It did not hit the governor! Is that possible? If it hit the governor, is it possible to be found in pristine condition? These are the questions that resulted from the "single bullet theory."

Photograph Composition of Frames 223 and 225

If the Stemmons Freeway sign had not obstructed the view of Abraham Zapruder, both John Connally and President Kennedy would have appeared from behind the sign simultaneously. As it was, the president appeared one-ninth of a second after the Texas governor. It is fair to assume that a person's body cannot move far in a ninth of a second, therefore the president would have been in approximately the same position in Frame 223 behind the sign. Perhaps his hand would have been slightly lower.

In Frame 225 Governor Connally begins to turn in response to hearing the first shot, while President Kennedy in Frame 223 has not yet been struck by the first bullet. Dr. Perry's assumptions about a front entry wound on the president's throat and the position of the two men show that it was not possible for the first bullet to have missed Governor Connally if it was fired from above and behind the motorcade.

It is necessary to use only the credible evidence to determine which bullet struck whom. Since the "stretcher bullet" is not conclusive evidence to suggest that it was fired from the gun while it was located on the sixth floor, it should not be a part of ascertaining which bullet hit the governor. The three shots heard can aid in the credibility of only three shots being fired. If the first hit the president and caused him to clutch at his throat, as witnesses reported, the second hit the governor and the third hit the president. When relatively simple deductions are made from the testimony of the eyewitnesses and the members of the motorcade, the result provides us with an imaginary view of what happened as the shots were fired.

An Eyewitness Account

The first shot sounds like a firecracker. The President reaches for his throat and slumps, but is unable to speak as the bullet transversed his windpipe. The governor, hearing the shot, turns instinctively to see if he can see the president. He cannot so he turns to his right in another attempt but is struck in this turn by the second shot. Seconds pass and Mrs. Kennedy reaches to help her husband and yet another shot sounds. The third shot strikes only the president. Evidence exists of two gunmen in Dealey Plaza, not a lone assassin firing from the sixth floor of the Depository.

If it were this simple, the Warren Commission would have concluded that the second shot hit the governor. It wasn't and the Commission had a reason!

Chapter Five

Doctor? Doctor?

Perhaps the confusion of the trajectory of the bullets, which bullet hit which man, how many shots resulted in how many wounds, and what testimony should be given a higher degree of credibility began with Dr. Malcolm Perry, the attending physician at Parkland Memorial Hospital. If the observations of the doctors at Parkland Hospital were correct, there may have been plausible evidence to indicate the presence of a gunman in front of President Kennedy which would have caused the testimony which was disregarded by the Commission to be credible.

John Connally's Gunshot Wounds

Seated in front of John Kennedy, Texas governor, John Connally, suffered wounds sustained from one bullet. The medical evidence regarding this wound was specific in that the bullet entered his back, exited his chest just below the right nipple and continued on to strike the radius bone on the back of his right wrist. Since the wound in the chest was considerably larger than the wound in his back, it was determined by the Commission and the attending physicians that the back wound was the point of entry. The wound sustained to the wrist was determined to be caused by this same bullet, as the nature of this wound and the governor's posture when the bullet impacted provided a high degree of probability.

In testimony before the Commission, Governor Connally said, "...I know it penetrated from the back through the chest first. I assumed that I had turned as I described a moment ago, placing my right hand on my left leg, that hit my wrist, went out the center of my wrist, the underside, and then into my leg, but it might not have happened that way at all."

The governor did not realize until the next day that the bullet had pierced his body in three places and although he did not provide the

Commission with concise details beyond a question of a doubt as to the position of his wrist when the bullet transversed his chest he was certain of his position when the bullet entered his back (facing left center).

In testimony, the governor revealed, "...looking a little bit to the left of center, and then I felt like someone hit me in the back." If the governor is correct and he was facing left center when the bullet struck him from behind, his wrist would need to be aligned with his chest exit wound (below the right nipple) in order to receive damage from the bullet which entered his back.

The Warren Commission maintained that it could not re-create the exact position of the governor or the president.

The Report reads, "The alignment of the points of entry was only indicative and not conclusive that one bullet hit both men. The exact positions of the men could not be re-created; thus the angle could only be approximated."

If the Commission had tried to ascertain the position of the two men by using the Zapruder film, it would seem that it would have been a rational method to re-create both the origins of the bullets and their trajectories. Why was it not possible for the Commission to determine the exact position of the men? If the governor's testimony (facing left center) and the medical evidence (one bullet causing all his wounds) provided a candid account, would not the Zapruder film indicate if the governor was correct about his assumptions? Or would it not at least provide the Commission with information regarding which bullet of the three fired in Dealey Plaza actually struck the governor?

The controversy surrounding the wounds sustained by Governor Connally is obviously plausible evidence and leads us to believe that the Commission's research of the assassination was at best shoddy. We can recall that the Commission was not interested in determining which bullet struck the governor. "...it is not necessary to any essential findings of the Commission to determine just which bullet hit Governor Connally," and it "could not re-create the exact position of the men."

Presumably what the Commission would have you believe is that a preponderance of evidence indicated that Oswald acted alone and regardless of not being able to determine when the governor was hit, all the shots were fired from above and behind the motorcade. If the rifle shot heard by Governor Connally was indicative of being the location from which the shots came, where was the gunman who fired the shot that struck Governor Connally? And where was the gunman who inflicted the head wound on the president, which resulted in a violent backwards motion of his head and upper torso? Based on the testimony of Governor Connally, there were three assassins, not one!

The wounds sustained by Governor Connally provided little doubt to the Commission that the gunman who fired the shot which struck him was the Commission that the gunman who fired the shot which struck him was positioned at a location behind the governor. After President Kennedy had sustained damage from the first bullet sound, the Texas governor turned a full 120 degrees to his right away from the Depository. This turn ultimately placed the governor's wound of entrance in a position away from the trajectory line established by the FBI from the sixth floor window to the limousine. The evidence which describes the actual course of the bullet and the damage retained by it is revealed in a Parkland Memorial Hospital operation summary form.

This medical record of the wounds sustained by John Connally became know as Commission Exhibit #392. The Report reads, "...It was found that the wound of entrance was just lateral to the right scapula close to the axilla yet had passed through the latissimus dorsi muscle, shattered approximately ten cm. of the lateral and anterior portion of the right fifth rib and emerged below the right nipple."

The location of this wound in laymen terms according to this report would place the point of entry to the left of the armpit at a point beside the right shoulder blade in the area of the latissimus dorsi muscle. The armpit is located adjacent to the second and third ribs, yet the fifth rib sustained damage laterally to about ten centimeters or four inches in length. The wound of entrance was determined to be approximately three centimeters in its longest diameter and the wound of exit a ragged wound approximately five centimeters in its greatest diameter. The wound reported in the president's throat was three millimeters in size, somewhat smaller than the wound of entry sustained by the governor.

Recreating the Shooting

For a moment picture yourself aiming a rifle out of the sixth floor window. The wind in Dallas is blowing approximately ten miles per hour and your goal as an assassin is to fire the rifle with precise accuracy. You must account for the velocity of the bullet as well as what a five to ten mile an hour wind speed can do to change its flight. You must calculate all the variables and consider the speed of the motorcade. The wind is likely to cause the bullets to sway from the target and their velocity will diminish as the bullets reach their destination and are likely to drop inches from the desired sight point. Only if your rifle is a quality-made weapon will your chances to strike your target be increased.

If the first shot does not cause sufficient damage, a second and possibly third will be necessary. Presumably your target is only the president. Therefore if you don't miss the first time, the accuracy could prove to be greater as you don't have to search for yet another target if you do miss.

By looking down on the plaza at the passing motorcade, you can assume that if your target is the president, the bullet is likely to continue on after striking the president, hitting the governor seated in front of the president. Now ask yourself a simple question. What prevented John Connally from simply agreeing with the Commission that one bullet struck both he and the president? Would it have made the event more understandable? (See Frame–225 FBI reenactment photo–View from Depository.) Notice when examining the FBI reenactment of Frame 225, the view through the rifle scope shows that the trajectory of this shot would have caused Governor Connally to sustain a wound to his lower back and that the bullet would more likely have struck the back of the car seat first.

In the Zapruder film, we can locate the governor as he begins to turn back to the left. Noting and agreeing for now that when the bullet struck him, he was facing left center. In the Zapruder film from the moment the president shows sign of being hit, we can examine the position of the governor and conclude beyond a reasonable doubt the following:

(1) which bullet struck him;

(2) the position he was in when he was struck;

(3) describe his reactions to the bullet passing through his body;

(4) establish a trajectory from the president's wounds.

If the bullet, as medical evidence indicated, struck his wrist, it will be apparent from viewing the film since an extremity such as a forearm and wrist could not retain its position after being impacted by a relatively high velocity bullet. Though the governor's wounds proved to be less serious than those sustained by President Kennedy, he was nevertheless shot in Dealey Plaza.

The Commission Report reads, "Based on his observations during the reenactment and the position of the Governor shown in the Zapruder film after the car emerged from behind the sign, Frazier testified that Governor Connally was in a position during the span from frame 207 to frame 225 to receive a bullet which would have caused the wounds he actually suffered. Governor Connally viewed the film and testified that he was hit between frames 231 and 234. According to Frazier, between frames 235 and 240 the Governor turned sharply to his right, so that by frame 240 he was to far to the right to have received his injuries at that time."

Since the FBI reported that President Kennedy showed clear signs of being struck at Frame 225, Connally could not have been hit later, if the shot were fired from the Depository, as the velocity of the bullet exceed eighteen hundred feet per second.

The assumptions of the Commission did not provide conclusive proof of which frame in the Zapruder film the governor actually sustained his injuries. In Frame 240 when he is facing the car door (according to the Commission), the governor was turned too far to the right. This fact was

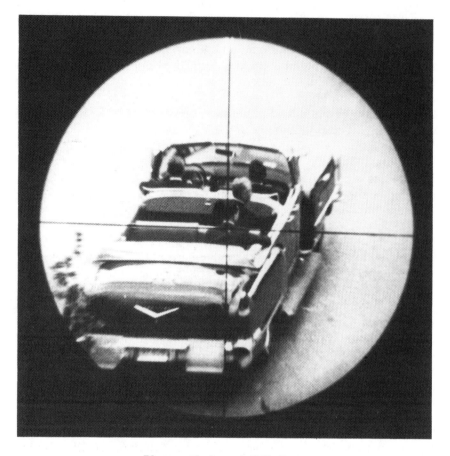

Photograph through Rifle Scope

Commission Exhibit #895

The FBI determined that President Kennedy showed clear signs of being hit at Frame 225, however the view through the rifle scope provided it with confusing alternatives.

The bullet, after passing through the President, would have continued on to strike the governor on his left side had he been in the position reenacted by the FBI. Though the view provided only plausible evidence of a single bullet striking both men, Governor Connally's wounds treated at Parkland Memorial Hospital clearly prevented it. (Photograph courtesy of Assassination Archives and Research Center.)

based *only* on the evidence of a gunman firing from the sixth floor of the Depository. If the governor was struck after this point (Frame 240), the Commission would have had to conclude that a second gunman was stationed on the south side of Elm Street or at a location consistent with inflicting the damage he suffered. The Zapruder film is the hard evidence and must be used to ascertain which shot hit Governor Connally.

If it were determined that the governor was hit later than Frame 240, the Commission's "single bullet theory" would be defeated.

Eyewitness Accounts of Governor Connally's Back Wound

The initial reports regarding the location of the back wound sustained by Governor Connally provide a confusing concept to the Official Report, which indicated that Connally's wounds were caused by the bullet which pierced the president's throat. While witnesses at Parkland Hospital reported to press reporters eager to send word of the circumstances of the shooting to their readers and listening audience, officials involved in the task of compiling reports gave their accounts. When the first report of Governor Connally's condition was announced by the attending physician at Parkland Hospital, a brief description was given as a probable account of what might have happened in Dealey Plaza. It was assumed that Governor Connally was in a sitting position (which he was) and that the bullet entered his back, exited his chest, and then continued in a downward angle to strike his wrist which was resting on his lap. The gunman, according to the first reports, was firing from above and behind the motorcade. This was only speculation at the time, but it became the official version.

A Reason to Believe

If Governor John B. Connally of Texas had not been shot in Dallas on 22 November, 1963, I can assure you that the assassin *would have been* captured and today you would know the truth about the event. The investigation into the president's death took a drastic turn when they learned the truth about the wounds sustained by the governor. If the bullet which struck the governor could not be linked to the sixth floor assassins window, an assassination attempt with two shooters would have been deemed highly probable. The evidence set forth by the FBI regarding John Connally's back wound can be questioned as to its credibility, in lieu of the inconsistencies which appear in testimony, eyewitness accounts, and photographs taken in Dealey Plaza.

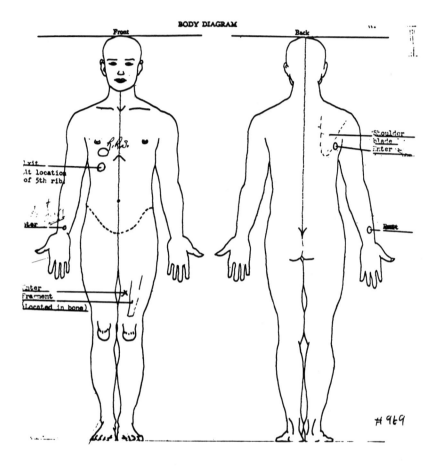

BODY DIAGRAM

Front   Back

Commission Exhibit #679

Governor John B. Connally

While these drawings (Commission Exhibits #679 and #680) indicate the locations of the governor's near fatal wounds, the point of entry shown here remains inconsistent with what eyewitnesses reported seeing. The Abraham Zapruder film also provides that John Connally's wound was eight inches lower and remains consistent with what Bill Stinson and Hurchel Jacks reported, "in the back below the shoulder blade." (See arrow.) (Drawing courtesy of Assassination Archives and Research Center.)

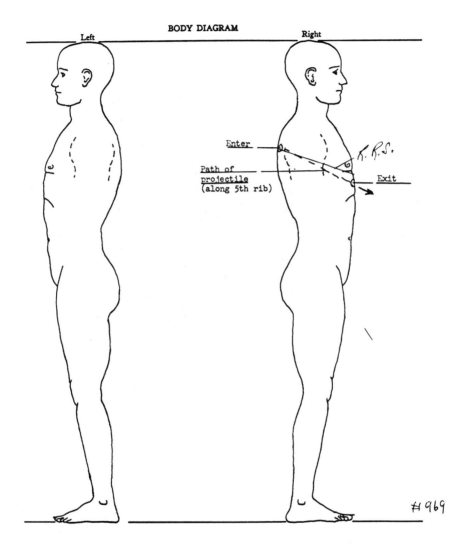

Commission Exhibit #680
Governor John B. Connally (Drawing courtesy of Assassination Archives and Research Center.)

Commission Exhibit #684
John Connally's jacket. (Photo courtesy of Assassination Archives and Research Center.)

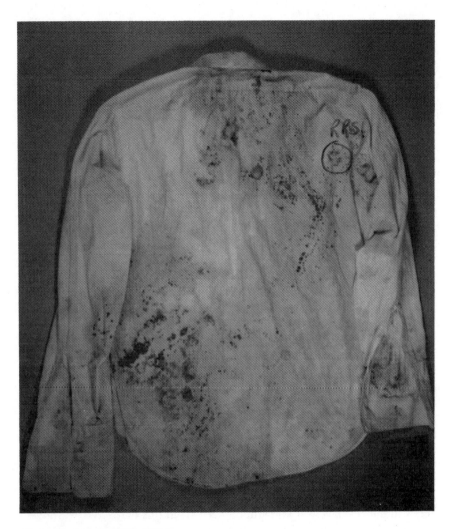

Commission Exhibit #685

John Connally's shirt.

The jacket and shirt which should have been taken from the Connallys at Parkland Hospital were retreived several weeks later. According to J. Edgar Hoover the holes could have been made by a bullet. However these articles were laundered. Why the holes in the jacket remain inconsistent with the location of which eyewitnesses reported seeing John Connally's wound of entrance cannot be determined by any available evidence other than Frame 345 of the Zapruder film. (Photo courtesy of Assassination Archives and Research Center.)

In Commission Exhibits #679 and #680, a wound of entrance is shown on a sketch drawing of John Connally's back. According to the FBI, this wound was located next to the shoulder blade, but near the arm pit. The bullet that caused this reported wound of entrance continued on to tear out ten lateral centimeters of John Connally's (anterior) fifth rib and then exited below the right nipple. According to the available medical evidence regarding this wound, it is unclear exactly where this bullet struck him, though examination of the clothing worn by John Connally on the day of the assassination (See Commission Exhibit #684 and #685) confirms the location of this wound.

Witnesses at Parkland Hospital, however, provided a detailed description of Governor Connally's wound of entrance, which remains as obscure by the Official Report as was the description of an entrance wound in President Kennedy's Adam's apple. While the witnesses have credibility and served in an official role the day of the assassination, to this day their reports have not been substantiated. The firsthand information the press delivered was deemed inaccurate by the Commission and the reports offered by officials on the scene were considered unreliable and not worthy of consideration.

Hurchel Jacks, a Texas state trooper and driver of the vice-presidential limousine in the motorcade, reported to the Commission his account upon reaching Parkland Hospital. "At the time the Secret Service Agents were removing Governor Connally from the jump seat. I could see that Governor Connally had been hit *just below the right shoulder blade in the back.*"

William Stinson, aide to Governor Connally, also saw the wound on the governor's back, although Stinson had talked with Governor Connally in the operating room. Stinson reported to Paul Healey of the *New York Daily News* that, "One bullet had ripped through Connally's back *just below the shoulder blade.*"

These accounts, which were eyewitness reports, file claim to a separate bullet striking Governor Connally at a much lower point on his body than the Official Report indicates, yet how could the bullet which struck Governor Connally in the back after passing through Kennedy exit several inches higher in his chest and still be fired from the sixth floor window?

The observations of Jacks and Stinson are backed up by photographic evidence contained in the Zapruder film as Governor Connally rolls over onto the floor of the limousine, while Jacqueline Kennedy begins to climb onto the truck. In this frame we find evidence that the FBI's reporting of John Connally's back wound was inaccurate. In fact if what we are seeing in this frame is a bullet wound, many questions abound.

Zapruder Frame #345

While it appears that the Zapruder film backs up the claims of both Stinson and Jacks, who reported John Connally's wound of entrance to be in the back below the shoulder blade, the doctors at Parkland Hospital reported the wound to be in the shoulder next to the armpit area. The exit wound has not been questioned as to its location below the right nipple.

1. Why would the FBI place into exhibit a sketch showing John Connally's wound of entrance to be eight inches higher than it appears to be in the Zapruder film?
2. If the wound of entrance was actually lower, why didn't the FBI tell us?
3. Why would John Connally's clothing (which was given to Nellie Connally at Parkland Hospital and subsequently laundered before the FBI picked it up) expose a bullet hole in a location higher than the one we see on the Zapruder film? Why did the FBI wait so long to get the clothing from Nellie?
4. If the holes were consistent with the actual wounds when Mrs. Connally received the clothes, why when she returned them did they not match the bullet wounds sustained by her husband as described by the witnesses? (Re: Jacks and Stinson)
5. What did J. Edgar Hoover report regarding the clothing worn by John Connally on the day of the assassination?
6. If the eyewitnesses who reported seeing Governor Connally's back wound below the shoulder blade were correct, would it not also indicate that the cover up conspiracy began at Parkland Hospital, including the doctors?

After examining the clothing worn by John Connally, the Commission sent it to the FBI laboratory in Washington for examination. J. Edgar Hoover reported to Commission member, Lee Rankin, on 16 April, 1964 his findings. The validity of the information regarding the wounds sustained by John Connally and the actual location of his wound of entrance can not be verified by the available evidence.

Commission No. *827*

UNITED STATES DEPARTMENT OF JUSTICE
FEDERAL BUREAU OF INVESTIGATION

WASHINGTON 25, D.C.

April 16, 1964

By Courier Service

Honorable J. Lee Rankin
General Counsel
The President's Commission
200 Maryland Avenue, Northeast
Washington, D. C.

Dear Mr. Rankin:

Reference is made to your letter dated April 9, 1964, covering transmittal to the FBI Laboratory of Governor John Connally's coat, shirt, trousers and tie and requesting an examination of these items. The results of the examinations are set forth below.

For your information the coat has been designated C311, the trousers C312, the shirt C313 and the tie C314.

Each hole in Governor John Connally's coat, shirt and trousers has the general appearance of a bullet hole and could have been made by a bullet. No hole was found in the tie.

The hole in the back of the coat is approximately 1/4" by 5/8", being elongated in a horizontal direction. The elongation could be due to one or more of the following: (1) a bullet passed through the cloth at an angle to the surface, (2) the cloth was folded when a bullet struck, (3) the hole was made by a mutilated bullet or (4) a bullet struck sideways.

The hole in the front of the coat is approximately 3/8" in diameter and circular in shape.

The hole in the sleeve is approximately 3/8" by 5/8" being elongated in a horizontal direction. The elongation of this hole could be due to one or more of the aforementioned causes.

Commission Document #827
Letter from Hoover to Rankin (Page 1 of 2)
(Letter courtesy of Assassination Archives and Research Center.)

CD 827

Honorable J. Lee Rankin

It is to be noted that holes corresponding to the three holes referred to above were found in the shirt. Due to the excessive tearing of the cloth, none of these holes were well defined.

The hole in the left trouser leg is approximately 1/4" in diameter and roughly circular in shape.

It was determined from the locations of the holes in the coat and shirt that a bullet entering the back, passing undeflected through the body and leaving the front, would have passed through Governor Connally at an angle of approximately 35 degrees downward from the horizontal and approximately 20 degrees from right to left if he was sitting erect and facing forward at the time he was shot. These angles are such that it would have been possible for Governor Connally's right arm and left leg to have been in direct line with the projectile. Any change in Governor Connally's position would affect the angles set out above. The possibility should not be overlooked that garments can shift from their normal position on the body. There is no way of determining, from an examination of the clothing, whether such a bullet may have followed a straight line path or may have been deflected in the body.

Nothing was found to indicate which holes were entrances and which were exits. The coat, shirt and trousers were cleaned prior to their receipt in the Laboratory, which might account for the fact that no foreign deposits of metal or other substances were found on the cloth surrounding the holes. Further, no characteristic position of the fibers of the cloth around the holes, which is one of the factors considered in determining whether a hole is an entrance or an exit hole, was found. The sizes of the holes in the clothing do not necessarily aid in this determination since a hole can be enlarged if a bullet strikes at an angle, sideways or partially sideways, or if it passes through a fold in the cloth. Also, if a bullet is irregularly mutilated, an entrance hole could be larger than an exit hole.

It was not possible from an examination of the clothing to determine whether or not all of the holes were made by the same projectile or projectile fragments.

Sincerely yours,

J. Edgar Hoover

Enclosures (14)

- 2 -

Commission Document #827
Letter from Hoover to Rankin (Page 2 of 2)
(Letter courtesy of Assassination Archives and Research Center.)

President Kennedy's Gunshot Wounds

The Warren Report, thus far, has provided little credibility to ascertaining what actually happened in Dealey Plaza other than reporting that the wounds suffered by President Kennedy resulted in his death at Parkland Hospital. According to the Commission, the Bethesda Naval Hospital examiners reported locating the wounds of entry on the back of the president's body, yet researchers of the assassination and doctors at Parkland Hospital have concluded that the wounds of entry were on the front of the president's body. The Official Report regarded much of the information as not being essential to its findings and has time and time again, left open-ended conclusions with unsubstantiated facts.

We've learned that not only did the Commission not determine which bullet hit Governor Connally, it also failed to determine the bullet wound's exact location and did not provide sufficient evidence to indicate why the president's head snapped violently backwards. It, too, was unable, through analysis of the Zapruder film, to establish a specific frame in which the bullets made contact and could not determine why the bullet that struck the President missed Governor Connally. When the body arrived in Bethesda, an autopsy was performed by Drs. James Humes, J. Thornton Boswell, and Pierre Finck. The findings of the examination were reported to the Commission by a copy of the autopsy report. The report regarding the medical evidence given to the Commission by the Bethesda Naval Hospital official adds to the preponderance of evidence that suggests the wounds sustained by the president came from behind.

The Commission reviewed the evidence. The Report reads, "....the smaller hole in the rear of the President's skull was the point of entry and that the large opening on the right side of his head was the wound of exit. The smaller hole on the back of the President's head measured one-fourth of an inch by five-eights of an inch (6 by 15 millimeters)."

The wound of exit reported by the Bethesda officials was located in the front portion of the president's head. If the Bethesda officials were correct in their judgment, would not this bullet also have struck other occupants in the limousine?

In review of the Zapruder film, the president's head is tipped downwards. The bullet strikes and his head snaps backwards. If the bullet struck the president and exited where the blood and cerebral fluid become apparent in Frame 313, this bullet would have certainly hit the governor, based on the trajectory analysis from the sixth floor window conducted by the FBI.

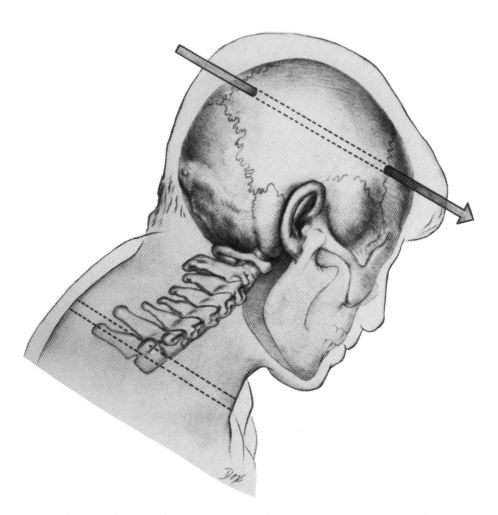

The Position of President Kennedy's Head
Reenactment of the Fatal Head Wound
The position of the president's head tipped downward with his chin nearly resting on his chest was not even considered by the Warren Commission in its reenactment of the fatal head shot. Note the rear entry location versus the front exit reported by the Commission. The motion of the president's head, which was propelled violently backwards, was not conclusive to determining the trajectory of this shot. (Drawing courtesy of Assassination Archives and Research Center.)

Frame 311—Position of President

The above photo shows the actual position of President Kennedy one-ninth of a second before the bullet made contact. In which direction the head moved has been clear for thirty years, however the trajectory established by the FBI from the sixth floor failed to determine why John Connally was not also struck by this bullet. It was not found in the car. Where did it go? The available medical evidence stands as front exit, rear entry.

The Commission Report continues, "The dimension of 6 millimeters, somewhat smaller than the diameter of a 6.5 bullet, was caused by the elastic recoil of the skull which shrinks the size of an opening after a missile passes through it."

If one can imagine a bullet traveling at a velocity of 2000 feet per second, striking a hard surface such as the skull, it is not conceivable that the point of entry would just open and close as the bullet passed through.

Notice, too, that the Report said, "The dimension of the 6 millimeters." The reference used by the Commission actually read, "6 by 15 millimeters." So how could it have shrunk? Its size was actually larger than the bullet that presumably caused it, yet the Commission concluded that it shrunk? Is that possible?

The following paragraph is found on page 86 of the Official Report. Without paraphrasing, the Report reads,

> The detail autopsy of President Kennedy performed on the night of 22 November at the Bethesda Naval Hospital led the three examining pathologists to conclude that the smaller hole in the rear of the President's skull was the point of entry and that the large opening on the right side of his head was the wound of exit. The smaller hole on the back of the President's head measured one-fourth of an inch by five-eights of an inch (6 by 15 millimeters). The dimensions of that wound were consistent with having been caused by a 6.5 millimeter bullet fired from behind and above which struck at a tangent or an angle causing a 15 millimeter cut. The cut reflected a larger dimension of entry than the bullet's diameter of 6.5 millimeters, since the missile, in effect, sliced along the skull for a fractional distance until it entered. The dimension of 6 millimeters, somewhat smaller than the diameter of a 6.5 millimeter bullet, was caused by the elastic recoil of the skull which shrinks the size of an opening after a missile passes through it.

If the opposite were true (Kennedy shot from the front), the bullet that struck the president's head transited from a point beginning approximately three and one-half inches above the right eyebrow. The larger portion of the wound was located in the parietal section of the skull. The skull portion did not break off and remained attached to the head, but shelved over to expose the right front area of the brain commonly referred as the area of the cerebral hemisphere. The detailing description of the autopsy report provides concise revelations of the path the bullet took, only if the shots were fired from behind.

Commission Exhibit #387, "Missile Wounds," reads,

1. There is a large irregular defect of the scalp and skull on the right involving chiefly the parietal bone but extends somewhat into the temporal and occipital regions. In this region there is an actual absence of scalp and bone producing a defect which measures approximately 13 cm. in greatest diameter.

   From the irregular margins of the above scalp defect tears extend in stellate fashion into the more or less intact scalp as follows:
   a. from the right inferior temporal-parietal margin anterior to the right ear to a point slightly above the tragus.
   b. from the anterior parietal margin anteriorly on the forehead to approximately 4 cm. above the right orbital ridge.
   c. from the left margin of the main defect across the midline antero-laterally for a distance of approximately 8 cm.
   d. from the same starting point as c. 10 cm. postero-laterally.

The description of the president's head wound is an exact reflection of the wound that appears on the Zapruder film. Nothing is mentioned in the autopsy report about the cerebellum being visible. In fact only the right cerebral hemisphere is visible. The autopsy report concluded that the brain was removed for further study.

One Wound—One Bullet

Though the autopsy examiners concluded that the "projectiles" were fired from above and behind the president, a preponderance of other evidence is conducive to determining that the bullets were fired from the front. What evidence suggests front entry? The head snap (back and to the left) is an indication and the position of the president's head when the bullet made contact is another. The fact that the bullet fragments remained in the skull and no bullet fragments relating to the president's head wound were found in the car is another. A description of the size of the fragments was made in the autopsy report as they were removed. "From the surface of the disrupted right cerebral cortex two small irregularly shaped fragments of metal are recovered. These measured 7 x 2 mm and 3 x 1 mm."

This indication provides us with evidence that the fragments were located on the surface of the brain, whereas the bullet penetrated the scalp (causing the shelving effect). The bullet fragmented and left only two small particles of lead.

The Zapruder film shows the rear of the president's head remaining intact. The only damage is on the front temporal margin extending into the parietal section, as noted in the autopsy examination. Drs. Humes and Boswell's determination of the head wound as being a result of a missile striking the president from behind had one serious flaw.

The doctors had not seen the Zapruder film and had no idea of the president's head responding as violently as it did to this bullet or the position of the president's head when this bullet made contact.

The conclusion of Lee Harvey Oswald acting alone is the major contributory element which has resulted in a distortion of the facts. If Oswald had fired three shots, the first would have knocked the president down and all the passengers in the car would have ducked. Instead we have the president grab first for his throat and then lurch forward as testified to by many witnesses in Dealey Plaza. This forward motion described can be best seen as a respiratory distress symptom.

The second bullet fired from the Depository, if it had hit the governor when he said it did; would have resulted in the bullet striking the back of the front seat where Secret Service Agent Roy Kellerman sat. Instead the bullet struck the governor leaving pieces in his wrist and on the car floor and fragments breaking off striking the limousine windshield on the inside causing Secret Service Agent William Greer to step on the brake for fear of gunfire coming from the front.

The third and fatal shot strikes the president from a point above and behind the motorcade, yet as we witness the Zapruder film (less the blood), it looks as if the president was just hit by a professional boxer. If it was from behind, we could expect even more fragments to be found in the car, yet there were only two. The one which hit the windshield (found the front seat) and another presumably under one of the jump seats, which did not come from either the first ("stretcher bullet") or the third bullet which was recovered from the president's body.

Evidence and Testimony

Certain evidence points to front entry wounds sustained by the president with the exception of Governor Connally being shot in the back at an undisclosed location between Frames 222 and 245 and the interpretation of the facts by those involved in the investigation.

Dr. Malcolm Perry reported the entrance wound in the Adam's apple to the press and began working on the president in efforts to save his life. If Perry had known the tracheotomy incision over the entry wound would obliterate the evidence of a frontal assault, perhaps it would have caused him to make the incision slightly higher. The size of the wound described by Perry was very small, in fact, smaller than the 6.5 millimeter exit wound we could expect if it had exited through the throat. Regardless Dr. Perry's performance was an indication that he had no intentions of withholding information regarding the assassination. Dr. Perry sent word to the press of an entry wound and the actions of the president provide conclusive proof that the bullet entered where the good doctor said it did, from the front.

The President's Back/Throat Wound

The autopsy report regarding the president's neck wound is detailed. The report reads, "The second wound presumably of entry is that described above in the upper right posterior thorax. Beneath the skin there is ecchymosis of the subcutaneous tissue and musculature. The missile path through the fascia and musculature cannot easily be probed. The wound presumably of exit was that described by Dr. Malcolm Perry of Dallas in the low anterior cervical region. When observed by Dr. Perry the wound measured 'a few millimeters in diameter,' however, it was extended as a tracheotomy incision and thus its character is distorted at the time of the autopsy. *However*, there is considerable ecchymosis of the strap muscles of the right side of the neck and of the fascia about the trachea adjacent to the line of the tracheotomy wound...."

The autopsy examination report did not question the validity of Dr. Perry's claim, in fact the report includes Perry's fundamental findings with the appearance of bruises (or ecchymosis) around the trachea and strap muscles. The appearance of bruises in the area that Dr. Perry described as being the location of a front entry wound indicates that an entry was probable. Had the bullet exited at this point, corresponding bruises may not have been visible since the damage would have originated from the interior of the thorax, not the exterior. The bruises were apparent in Bethesda as was the wound appearance in Dallas.

Official Autopsy Report Inconsistent with Photos

Naturally the Warren Commission concluded that the wounds sustained by President Kennedy on his head were the result of a bullet being fired from the Book Depository. The wound on the top of the president's head was about the size of an adult fist. It remained both attached and intact with the exception of a few fragments torn away as the bullet made contact. If one can visualize "opening a tin can partially, but leaving the lid attached," the president's head wound had similar visual qualities. The head wound located on the front of the president's head resembled both an exit and entrance wound, but where were the bullet fragments found?

The fragments were located on the surface of the brain (cerebral cortex). If the bullet had struck the president from behind at a velocity exceeding 1800 feet per second, the fragments would have been found closer to the front portion of the skull. Instead they were located on top. If the bullet that struck the president did enter from the front (re: head snap), the bullet would have fragmented upon impact. The scalp region, which remained attached, was on the right side of the head in the area above the ear. It is fair to conclude that the bullet's trajectory sliced off, but did not completely sever this portion of the scalp. The point of entry for this type of wound would be located at a point to the left front of the portion of the open wound if it were a result of a front entry wound.

According to research conducted by David Lifton in his book, *Best Evidence*, Malcolm Kilduff reported the president's *wound of entrance* to be located approximately one inch above and to the left of the right temple.

In the statement of Hurchel Jacks, researched by Josiah Thompson, Jacks indicated Connally's wound of entrance in a place inconsistent with the official version, also stated, "Before the President's body was covered up it appeared that *the bullet had struck him above the right ear or near the temple.*"

The Cover-Up

As we examine the official sketched autopsy drawing submitted to the Commission by Dr. J. Thornton Boswell, note the location of the back wound and the head wound in relation to the president's collar line. Now examine the president's jacket and shirt which show the entry hole for the back wound. It appears from this evidence that the back wound was located quite low. The head wound measured 6 x 15 millimeters and the back wound measured 7 x 4 millimeters.

It appears by examining the autopsy sketch that only two wounds are visible on the president's back. One to the left of his shoulder blade and the other is a horizontal line (near the occipital pertuberance) about midline of the skull. These wounds are a concise reflection of the official autopsy report offered to the Commission by Dr. Humes and Dr. Boswell. However when comparing the original autopsy drawing to the autopsy photographs (which were first published by David Lifton in *Best Evidence*, inconsistencies exist which can only be linked to a cover-up conspiracy.

While the autopsy report and the sketched drawing support the points of entry indicated from the official version regarding the president's wounds, the photograph of the rear of the president's head provides startling proof of a wound which was undetected in Dallas and presumably overlooked in Bethesda, but known to exist by the FBI. (See autopsy

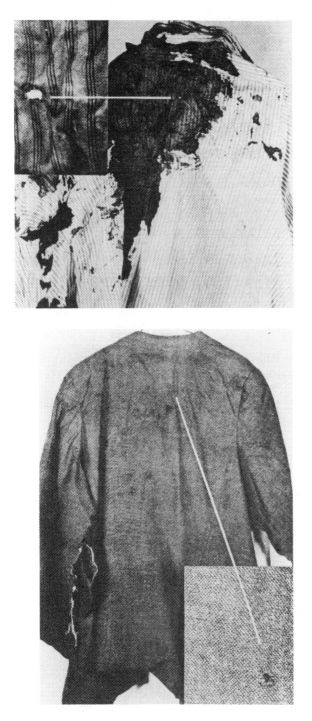

Shirt and Jacket Worn by President

The alignment of the hole in the president's jacket did not remain consistent with the wound located high on the back in the autopsy photos. It is plausible, however, that the clothing was bunched up, but we know the president was no slouch either. The wound at the base of the hairline seen in the autopsy photos was not caused when this hole was made. If this is a bullet hole, it would suggest that the president suffered from three gunshot wounds. But he did not. (Photograph courtesy of AP/Wide World Photos.)

drawing and photos.) It is improbable that the examining pathologist at Bethesda Naval Hospital overlooked what appears to be a wound at the base of President Kennedy's hairline when conducting the autopsy or even missed locating it while preparing the sketch.

If Dr. Malcolm Perry's observation of an entrance wound below the president's Adam's apple was correct, how is this wound (if it is a wound) related to a bullet fired from above and behind the president? Note also the back wound and its relative position to being in line with the trajectory analysis conducted by the FBI. The Bethesda examiners reported that the back wound began the track for the bullet which presumably entered the president's body in a twenty-degree downward angle and then exited the president's throat several inches higher. The probability that a cover-up of the facts began in Dallas can be substantiated by examination of the autopsy photos and raises many questions concerning the true validity of the autopsy report which was confirmed to be accurately worded by the Journal of the American Medical Association in June 1992.

The wound on the top of the president's head is not visible in the autopsy photos, but was pointed out in the autopsy sketch. Why is it not visible? Did the bullet which rocketed the president's head in a violent backwards motion exit the head? Or did the skull react more like a baseball glove catching a fast ball causing the violent and sudden backwards motion of the president's head?

The back wound does not appear to be consistent with causing a throat wound based on the trajectory study. Why? Was the president shot from the front or from behind?

A wound at the base of the hairline is present in the photos but was not indicated in the official autopsy report. Why didn't the government release this information? What are Drs. Humes and Boswell hiding from the American public? What did they see? Or what didn't they see?

The rear of the president's head appears to be intact here in the photos and in the Zapruder film, yet several Dallas doctors have indicated that the entire rear of the president's head was blown out. What are they trying to say? Why can't the Zapruder film substantiate a claim of the rear of the president's head being blown out?

In the full face photograph of President Kennedy, note the facial puffiness, the wide open eyes, and the neatness of his bangs. This photo was presumably taken ten hours after the president was pronounced dead at Parkland Memorial Hospital in Dallas. Based on this information, can we, beyond a reasonable doubt, concur that this photo was taken ten hours later in Bethesda? Think about it.

The FBI Challenge
to the Autopsy Report

If the mystery of the president's death is ever to be resolved, it will include the government's own challenge to the autopsy reports filed by Drs. Humes and Boswell. Here the wound at the base of the hairline has been marked with tape and the back wound with chalk. There is no evidence here of the rear head wound which was described by measurements and can be seen in the autopsy sketch. The throat wound described by Dr. Perry was a wound of entrance below the Adam's apple. If the FBI examined the clothing worn by the president, is the location here consistent with the autopsy sketch and not the clothing? (Photograph courtesy of Assassination Archives and Research Center.)

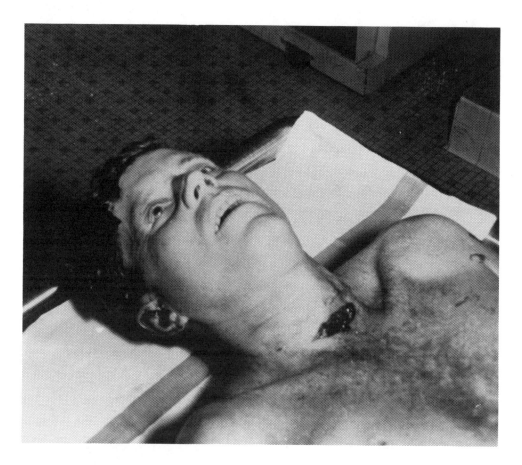

Autopsy Photo

This photograph was taken at Bethesda Naval Hospital nearly eight hours after the president was pronounced dead by doctors at Parkland Hospital in Dallas. Note the wide-eyed stare and facial puffiness.

The incision made by Perry is represented here. However any evidence of a front entry wound was lost when the incision was made in order to restore Kennedy's breathing. One can easily question the validity of when this photo was taken. (Photo courtesy of Mark A. Crouch, original source James K. Fox, U.S. Secret Service.)

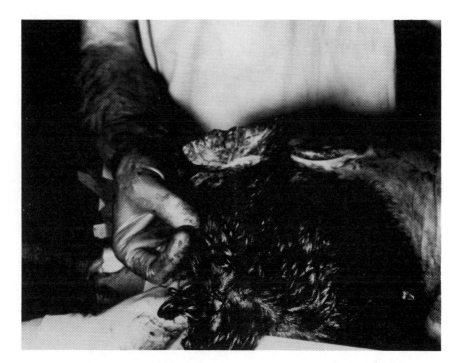

Autopsy Photo

As the photographer prepared to take this photo, the president was rolled over onto his side. One hand of the surgeon balanced his body at the shoulder while the other supported the top of his head.

Note the wound at the base of the hairline reenacted by the FBI when it used adhesive tape to mark the wound. This photo shows no wound of entry at the top of the head where Drs. Humes and Boswell reported finding one. (See autopsy sketch.) A hole measuring 6 x 15 millimeters would be detectable. Why the autopsy doctors failed to disclose the wound at the base of the hairline is unclear and raises the question if indeed they saw the president's body at all. If Perry was right about the entry wound, could the bullet have exited here? (Photo courtesy of Mark A. Crouch, original source James K. Fox, U.S. Secret Service.)

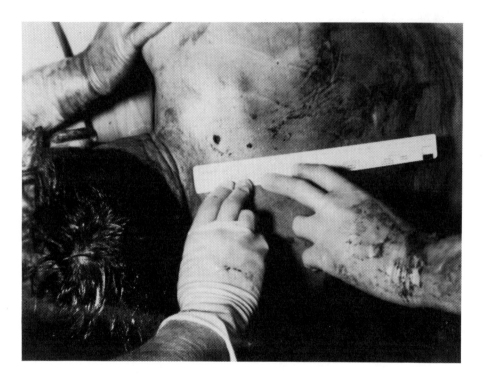

Autopsy Photo
Compare to the jacket and shirt worn by President Kennedy this photo disclosing the back wound. Determine the location of the bullet holes and the trajectory established by them. Just how far would the president's jacket and shirt have had to have been bunched up in order to create a wound at this location? Is it a wound? The back wound, barely distinguishable here, is located high up on the back closer to the shoulder. Two others present when the photos were taken hold the ruler which was used to measure the angle of trajectory for the throat wound. (Photo courtesy of Mark A. Crouch, original source James K. Fox, U.S. Secret Service.)

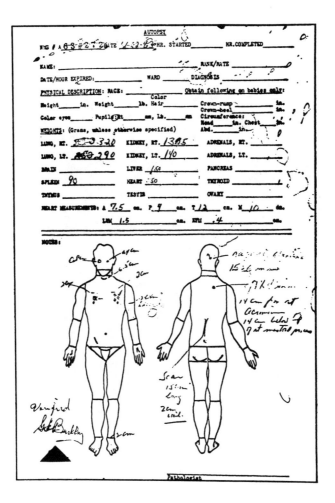

Commission Exhibit #397

The FBI questioned the validity of the autopsy as opposed to the actual wounds suffered by the president simply because the wounds shown in the autopsy were not disclosed to the Warren Commission.

Here the original autopsy sketch stained with blood does not disclose the wound at the base of the hairline used in the trajectory analysis study conducted by the FBI. In the June 1992 issue of the Journal *of the American Medical Association, the autopsy surgeons were commended for the job they did, as the Journal reported that, "the President was struck by two and only two bullets from behind." I doubt that the Journal's editor even examined the autopsy photos showing the wound at the base of the hairline not found in this final report. (Drawing courtesy of Assassination Archives and Research Center.)*

Kennedy at Fort Worth

This photograph of President Kennedy was taken in Fort Worth on the morning of the assassination. This photo shows the President's full head of hair with wide sideburns cut evenly horizontal with his eyes, as well as hair grown down tightly next to his ear. This is a very good picture of President John F. Kennedy. Compared to the full face photo of the president taken at Bethesda Naval Hospital, it appears that much of the hair near his right ear had been removed that evening. There was no mention in the Official Report given to President Johnson of the Bethesda examiners cutting any hair. (Photo courtesy of UPI/Bettmann.)

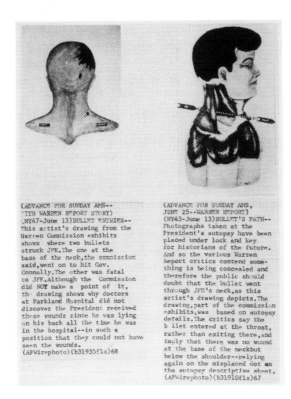

Artist Drawings with News Releases
(Photograph courtesy of AP/Wide World Photos.)

Why Won't They Tell the Truth?

The Warren Commission would have us believe that its version is infallible and cannot be changed, yet the evidence that tells us of a very different story in Dallas remains in the "negative file" created by the Commission. If the Zapruder film, the autopsy photos, the autopsy examination, and the eyewitness testimony remain confusing, we must determine the reasons and motives behind the Warren Commission concluding that all the shots in Dallas were fired from the Depository.

The Warren Commission's Official Report has been a disservice to this nation and perhaps the world. Its far-reaching conclusions distorted the very evidence that the assassination researchers regard as credible evidence indicating the presence of other gunman in the plaza. The Zapruder film is regarded as the single piece of credible evidence available to the researchers. Along with the autopsy photos, the eyewitness testimony, and other relevant information, the film produces detail of the most shocking event in history.

A conspiracy to take the life of the president can be found in the form of hard evidence and the Warren Commission, though it did not take part in the actual conspiracy to take John Kennedy's life, in my opinion, took part in a government conspiracy to keep the truth from us. It lodged a conspiracy of its own, presumably to safeguard the facts and prevent interference with preestablished lines of prosecution and though the Warren Commission had the best interest of the people in mind, it failed to produce the results necessary to disclosing the truth about the president's death.

The Warren Commission was responsible for ascertaining the facts submitted by the doctors of Parkland and the examiners of Bethesda Naval Hospital. Many inconsistencies exist and provide researchers with substantial proof that the Commission's findings were inconclusive to determining with a reasonable doubt that the shots which were fired came from the 6.5 millimeter rifle in the Depository building behind the motorcade. The evidence of the entry wounds sustained by both the governor and the president cannot be dismissed or regarded as being caused by something or from somewhere that simply could not have caused them.

Just as the three centimeter entry wound in Governor Connally's back could not have come from a 6.5 millimeter bullet; the evidence of a three millimeter entry wound in the president's throat cannot be linked to an exit wound of a 6.5 millimeter bullet which would have left at least an eight millimeter hole as it exited. The head wound, determined to be front entry by the Zapruder film, cannot be regarded as rear entry with the bullet fragments being found in the cerebral hemisphere of the brain simply because, the 6 x 15 millimeter entry wound described by Drs. Humes and Boswell cannot be seen in the official autopsy photos. With no rear exit found for this particular wound, could it have been fired from behind? Of course not!

Chapter Six

Back to the Future

Picture yourself for a moment riding in the motorcade through the streets of Dallas with Vice President Johnson. The car you are riding in is approximately forty-five feet behind the presidential limousine. The car will not stop and it will take you onto Elm Street and through Dealey Plaza. You will hear three shots fired, presumably at the presidential limousine, but you have no way of telling. You will not be able to see anyone actually struck by the bullets, but will feel the anxiety and frustration felt by many in Dallas that afternoon. The car will proceed through the plaza and take you to Parkland Memorial Hospital where the president is treated and pronounced dead.

The vision of the assassination that you are about to explore is not much different from what Senator Ralph Yarborough of Texas and many others relived for many months following the assassination in Dallas. Perhaps the trauma of that event will remain with them forever. Being an eyewitness of the assassination was not a pleasant experience and will never be forgotten. For some of us, the recollections of the event may fade, but for those who were actually in the plaza on 22 November, 1963, they may never be free of the memory of those few short seconds. Witnessing an event as tragic as the death of President Kennedy was without question traumatic, yet as time passes it may erase many unwanted memories.

Whatever did happen in Dallas, happened, and it will not change the way you felt about the president's untimely death. It will not bring John Kennedy back to us, but perhaps understanding the truth will release this heavy burden from us. The truth is John Kennedy never left us. He is here in our hearts and it is here we have kept him all these years. John Kennedy will always be remembered as the young president whose career ended shortly after it began.

If the truth about John Kennedy's death is ever completely understood by the public, the controversy that has remained to this day will be accounted for. There must be a reason for researchers of the event to have

111

fostered doubt in the minds of many millions of people that the assassination was *not* the result of one crazy person in a book depository who felt he was serving justice to his country. Evidence exists that others were involved and that a conspiracy did take place, yet who these people were remains the question.

From looking into *Mirror of Doubt*, we've seen that photographic alterations began a conspiracy to thwart the facts. The alterations were part of a well planned attempt to not only convince the general public that the shots were fired from above and behind the motorcade but also to confuse the eyewitnesses present in Dealey Plaza. When an eyewitness reported that he saw a rifle sticking out of the sixth floor window, the Dallas police soon emerged with a rifle. It is probable that anyone who was in the plaza at that time of the shooting stayed around long enough to witness the first piece of credible evidence in the Kennedy assassination case being carried out of the building.

The facts published by the Warren Commission denote the possibility of another gunman being located in Dealey Plaza. There are other facts about the assassination that the Warren Commission failed to report in the official version, facts that tell a very different story. What happened in Dealey Plaza?

The evidence that began my research into the event I did not find in the Warren Commission's Official Report and it is just as unclear today as it was then, why the Commission did not disclose or even record this information. The implications alone have provided me with insight into the assassination and brought to life evidence discounted by many for reasons of doubt. Why the Commission ruled the way it did may never be determined, yet it is clear after thirty years, it regarded those facts as "negatives." Remember that a theory must be proven beyond the means of reasonable doubt. *Mirror of Doubt* does not promote theories. It is based on evidence and facts documented by the Warren Commission, and facts and testimony overlooked by it. *Mirror of Doubt* has not drawn theories or regarded anything that can not be substantiated. If it has in error, it has raised questions. It has on the basis of the facts reached a conclusion which can be substantiated.

What you are about to learn will not surprise you. A friend of mine who discussed the assassination and my findings with me on one occasion told me, "Whatever does come out this time; will be it, regardless if its the truth; or not." I for one believe him, but I do feel that the results will be guaranteed by the many researchers and law enforcement people who have recently learned the truth and are willing to continue to investigate the implications of a cover-up conspiracy. When I first began my research, it took me about one week to resolve the puzzling doubts pertaining to the mystery of Dallas 1963. This told me that I was not alone and that many people had *solved* the murder of the president. Researchers such as David

Lifton, Jack White, Jim Marrs, Jim Moore, Josiah Thompson, Harrison Livingstone, Jim Garrison, and Robert Groden are among the most talked about professionals. These men have devoted their entire lives to breaking the backs of the conspirators and inspiring the truth. Oliver Stone's movie *JFK* is just one of the inspired works. But there is a difference between solving something and proving it.

The credit for inspiration of my research goes to Paul Healey, a staff news correspondent for the *New York Daily News*. Mr. Healey reporting from Dallas on the day of the assassination. His report can be found in the *New York Daily News*, dated 23 November, 1963, the day after the assassination.

The Truth About Dealey Plaza

Once again picture yourself riding in the presidential motorcade. As the vice-presidential limousine travels through Dealey Plaza, you hear three shots. At the time of the first shot, you are approximately forty-five feet behind the president. A Secret Service car blocks your view, but you make every attempt to try to see if you can see anything unusual. The Secret Service agent riding in the front seat of your car will also hear the shot. Almost immediately a second shot sounds! The Secret Service agent plunges into the back seat in an attempt to protect you and the others from harm. The third shot rings out. In the course of the next hour, the president of the United States will be pronounced dead.

A statement given to Paul Healey by Senator Ralph Yarborough of Texas appeared in the *New York Daily News* on 23 November, 1963. This one statement provided me with enough insight and determination to bring to the public *Mirror of Doubt* and locate the "negatives" experienced by the Warren Commission. The conclusions you draw will be your own. Was there a government cover-up conspiracy? Was there a lone assassin?

Statement Given by Senator Ralph Yarborough of Texas

"It is too horrible to describe. We did not see them shot but we knew immediately they were. I saw a Secret Service man in the car beating his fists on the back as they drove off in frustration, anger and despair.

"There was one shot," Yarborough went on, "a pause, another shot, a longer pause, and then the third shot. The first two shots were fairly close together.

"The smell of gunpowder was so strong you could smell it all the way back were we were."

The smell of gunpowder, Yarborough described was witnessed by several other witnesses in the general vicinity of the president's car. Presumably the Warren Commission failed to substantiate why a predominant odor of gunpowder lingered in the plaza air just as the shots were ringing out. There was a strong south wind in Dealey Plaza at the time of the assassination attempt and it carried the smell up into the railroad yard behind the grassy knoll, which was located to the north of the motorcade route.

Though this evidence did not remain in Dealey Plaza for long, it was nevertheless smelled by more than one witness. There were no firecrackers set off, only gunshots which bore resemblance to the sounds created by firecrackers. The smell of gunpowder was linked directly to the shots as they were being fired.

The Dallas mayor's wife, Mrs. Earle Cabell, riding two cars behind Ralph Yarborough, also in an open limousine, testified before the Warren Commission. She said, "I was acutely aware of the odor of gunpowder."

Too, when asked by Mr. Hubert of the Commission if she made the observation to anyone at the time about the gunpowder smell, she replied, "No; because there was too much confusion. But I mentioned it to Congressman Roberts a couple of weeks ago." She was then asked if he had smelled the gunpowder. She said, "As well as I remember he said 'Yes.' We were in a group, a large group, and there was much conversation."

This account as well as all of the testimonies reported here, was not found in the Official Report on the President's Commission on the Assassination of President Kennedy. In fact you cannot find testimony in the Official Report that would contradict the conclusion of the Warren Commission that Lee Harvey Oswald acted alone.

Diagram 7

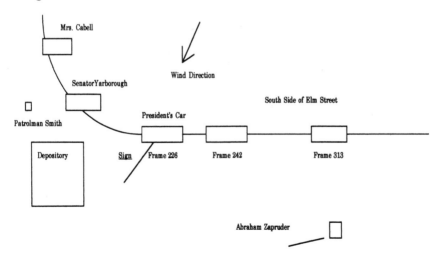

Senator Yarborough issued a letter to the Commission that was submitted with a copy of a photo taken by an Associated Press photographer
working in Dallas, James Altgens. Senator Yarborough does not mention
the word "gunpowder" and indicated in his official testimony that the shots
appeared to come from the right behind him. On the basis of the other
testimonies here and the recorded statement indicating that gunpowder
was smelled on the plaza, I must conclude that for whatever reason he
chose, Yarborough was careful about what he told the Commission or his
testimony was simply kept from the public.

Given Yarborough's location at the time the shots were fired, what does
the smell of gunpowder indicate about the scene? How does Yarborough's
affidavit differ from the account recorded by Paul Healey in Dallas a short
time after the assassination?

Affidavit of Ralph W. Yarborough

President's Commission
on the Assassination of
President John F. Kennedy   Affidavit

In response to the oral request of one of the attorneys for the
Commission that I send you an affidavit for inclusion in the
record of the assassination of President John F. Kennedy, I make
the following statement:

On November 22, 1963, as the President and Mrs. Kennedy
rode through the streets of Dallas, I was in the second car behind
them. The first car behind the President's car was the Secret
Service car; the second car behind them was Vice-President
Lyndon Johnson's car. The driver and secret service agent were
on the front seat of the Vice-President's car. Vice-President
Lyndon B. Johnson sat on the right side of the rear seat of the
automobile, Mrs. Lyndon B. Johnson was in the center of the
rear seat, while I sat on the left side of the rear seat.

After the Presidential motorcade had passed through the
heart of downtown Dallas, experiencing an exceptionally warm
and friendly greeting, as the motorcade went down the slope of
Elm Street toward the railroad underpass, a rifle shot was heard
by me; a loud blast, close by. I have handled firearms for fifty
years, and thought immediately that it was a rifle shot. When
the noise of the shot was heard, the motorcade slowed to what
seemed to me a complete stop (though it could have been a near
stop). After what I took to be about three seconds, another shot

boomed out, and after what I took to be one-half the time between the first and second shots (calculated now, this would have put the third shot about one and one-half seconds after the second shot—by my estimate—to me there seemed to be a long time between the first and second shot, a much shorter time between the second and third shots—these were my impressions that day), a third shot was fired. After the third shot was fired, the cavalcade speeded up, gaining speed rapidly, and roared away to Parkland Hospital.

I heard three shots and no more. All seemed to come from my right rear. I saw people fall to the ground on the embankment to our right, at about the time of or after the second shot, but before the cavalcade started up and raced away.

Due to the second car, with the secret service men standing on steps on the sides of it, I could not see what was happening in the Presidential car during the shooting itself. Some of the secret service men looked backward and to the right, in the general direction from which the rifle explosion seemed to come.

After the shooting, one of the secret service (men) sitting down in the car in front of us pulled out an automatic rifle or weapon and looked backward. However, all of the secret service men seemed to me to respond very slowly, with no more than a puzzled look. In fact, until the automatic weapon was uncovered, I had been lulled into a sense of false hope for the President's safety, by the lack of motion, excitement, or apparent visible knowledge by the secret service men, that anything so dreadful was happening. Knowing something of the training that combat infantrymen and Marines receive, I am amazed at the lack of instantaneous response by the Secret Service, when the rifle fire began. I make this statement in this paragraph reluctantly, not to add to the anguish of anyone, but it is my firm opinion, and I write it out in the hope that it might be of service in the better protection of our Presidents in the future.

After we went under the underpass, on the upward slope I could see over the heads of the occupants of the second car (Secret Service Car) and could see an agent lying across the back or truck of the Presidential car, with his feet to the right side of the car, his head at the left side. He beat the back of the car with one hand, his face contorted by grief, anguish, and despair, and I knew from that instant that some terrible loss had been suffered.

<u>On arrival at the hospital, I told newsmen that three rifle shots had been fired. There was then no doubt in my mind that the shots were rifle shots, and I had neither then or now any</u>

doubts that any other shots were fired. In my opinion only three
shots were fired.

The attached photograph from pages 24 and 25 of the
Saturday Evening Post of December 14, 1963, shows the motorcade, as I remember it, an instant after the first shot. [Photo-
graph is Yarborough Exhibit A.]

Given and sworn to this 10th day of July, 1964, at Washington, District of Columbia.

Signed this 10th daily of July 1964
(signed) Ralph W. Yarborough
Ralph W. Yarborough

Senator Yarborough's account differs greatly from what he told the
news reporters at Parkland Hospital. In his official affidavit his response
to what he told the reporters sounds more like a retraction to please the
Warren Commission staffers than telling the truth. Did Yarborough smell
gunpowder? Mrs. Cabell and Congressman Roberts indicated in testimony
that they had, yet they were two cars behind Yarborough.

One other witness, according to my research, smelled gunpowder and
by it I have determined that many more may have also smelled it but did
not reflect it in testimony or the testimony has been kept from the
American public and perhaps even Congress (the Secret Service agents in
particular). The account of Joe Marshall Smith was reported by David
Lifton in his book, *Best Evidence*. Patrolman Smith was directing traffic at
the corner of Houston and Elm Streets. When he heard three shots (which
have been reported to have come from the area west of the Depository),
he ran immediately to that area and followed people into the railroad yard
where he caught the smell of gunpowder in the air. The smell of gunpowder
may not have been conclusive to determining exactly where the shots came
from at the time of the shooting, but combined with the testimony of other
witnesses in the plaza, it is conducive to determining that the shots could
not have come from the Depository. If these accounts have any credibility,
we would need to have other evidence to form some sort of an opinion as
to the source of the shots.

It is inconceivable that the smell of gunpowder could have escaped so
rapidly from the inside the sixth floor window of the Depository and be
smelled by members of a motorcade which presumably did not come to a
complete stop. Too if an expert in the field of firearms was asked his
opinion as to determining what the odor of gunpowder would indicate, he
would reply that the shots were more likely to be much closer than

seventy-five feet in the air, vertical to the motorcade on the street below.

The sounds of the shots were nearly unanimous in that they were recalled as being like firecrackers or motorcycles backfiring. Perhaps this question, too, can be asked to those knowledgeable of firearms. This clue to the assassination began with puzzling doubts and unanswered questions.

Senator Yarborough's car did not stop, yet as the shots rang out the momentary pauses yielded to an odor of gunpowder! Other witnesses reported smelling it as well.

The Depository Theory—You Decide

The Warren Commission's conclusion was based primarily on the evidence of a 6.5 millimeter rifle and three empty cartridges recovered by the Dallas police a short time after the assassination. It was later reported that an eyewitness actually described a man, whom he said was visible for a short time as the shots were being fired from the Depository. This account subsequently led to the arrest of Lee Harvey Oswald, a Book Depository worker who had watched the motorcade pass by the building. Did Oswald fire these shots? Could any of the shots have come from the Book Depository?

On the southeast corner of the Depository, the sixth floor window was opened only eighteen inches. A photo taken by Thomas C. Dillard shows the open window and two depository workers standing in the windows one floor below. A corner of the box, presumably used as a gun rest, is visible. One of the men on the fifth floor appears to be looking towards the area of the motorcade just west of the building, while the other looks towards the crowd stationed along Houston Street in the direction of Dillard. These men were eyewitnesses to the assassination, as were the many on the street below. Their testimonies were taken and appear in the official version of the Warren Commission's report.

According to the Commission, Dillard took two photos (Commission Exhibits C and D) of the building as or just after the shots were fired. Dillard's photos show no one standing in the sixth floor window, but they are conclusive evidence that the window was open. (But how far?) Several witnesses reported seeing a "pipe" or a "rifle" sticking out of the window after the shots were fired, according to the Commission.

Standing nearly one hundred feet away, another eyewitness reported seeing a man he later described to police, "resting against the left window sill, with gun shouldered to his right shoulder." Though many witnesses reported seeing many things, it was later proven that mistakes were made. Even the Commission argued the possibility of a gunman leaning against the window, as it was photographed during the shooting (according to witnesses), partially closed. The description the man gave to police did not match the description of Lee Harvey Oswald but was the eyewitness account that led to the arrest of Oswald.

The Commission reported that Brennan (the eyewitness who gave the police a description of Oswald) was mistaken. The half-open window and the arrangement of boxes would have precluded the account of the gunman standing and lurching out the window. The angle of the shots, too, virtually precluded this possibility. Later when Brennan was asked to identify the person in the window, he chose Oswald from a police line-up, but stated he could not make a positive identification. The clothing worn by Oswald at the time of his arrest did not match the light brown shirt described by Brennan. If the single bullet, lone gunman ruling of the Commission was even remotely accurate, the gunman would have had to lean out the window in order to fire the missiles and match the trajectory of the president's first wound. The partially closed window prohibited it!

The mystery of Dealey Plaza does not surround the eyewitnesses who reported hearing shots being fired from the sixth floor window or even the eyewitness account that led Dallas authorities to arrest Oswald. It lies in the unprecedented smell of gunpowder that the Warren Commission chose to regard as a "negative" and the testimony of those who had a general idea where the sound of the shots came from.

Firecracker Noises

According to the Warren Commission's report, many of the witnesses related the sound of the shots to motorcycles backfiring or firecrackers being thrown. The origin of the three shots could not be accurately determined because of the acoustical design of the plaza, yet the smell of gunpowder was dismissed. It is apparent that the evidence against Lee Harvey Oswald was more than just circumstantial. In fact based on the photographic evidence and the testimony of the arresting officers who interrogated Oswald, the evidence against him was circumstantial. Three empty cartridges were found, three shots were heard, and a smell of gunpowder was testified to by Ralph Yarborough and others.

Consider for a moment the shots being fired from the sixth floor window. One does not need to be a firearms expert to detail the sound of a bullet exiting a gun. If it is a low caliber weapon, the sound would be like a pop or a crack. A rifle shot to the hunters of this world sets ringing in the ears. The result of a high-powered rifle fired from within a building would muffle. The sound would not carry. It would sound like an explosion and be contained. It would immediately draw the attention of anyone standing in close proximity to the Depository.

Now consider the rifle being fired three consecutive times from the sixth floor window. If so much as one shot was fired, it would have been heard and regarded as explosive noise, not as firecrackers or motorcycles backfiring, and all the witnesses in the plaza would have concurred. The three shots would have been linked immediately to the building above and no controversy would exist today. These are the sounds that were heard and were unrelated to what a rifle being fired from inside a tall building would sound like. If we conclude that the third shot hit the president from the front, an additional shot fired from the Depository would have given the witness two separate yet distinct locations of shots being fired. We must also conclude that one of the empty cartridges was planted by the conspirators.

Victoria Adams, a Depository worker, testified that her view was obstructed by a tree. Adams, watching the passing motorcade from the fourth floor window of the Depository, reported to the Commission, "And we heard a shot, and it was a pause, and then a second shot, and then a third shot." (Notice the similarity to what Yarborough heard.) "It sounded like a firecracker or a cannon at a football game, it seemed as if it came <u>from the right below</u> rather than from the left above."

Ronald Fischer, employed as an auditor of the city of Dallas, reported hearing three shots. Fischer testified, "Well, as I looked around to watch these other cars, I heard a shot. At first *I thought it was a firecracker*. And—uh—everybody got quiet. There was no yelling or shouting or anything. Everything seemed to get real still. And—uh—*the second shot rang out*, and then everybody—from where I was standing—everybody started to scatter. And—uh—*then the third shot*."

Fischer was standing on the south side of Elm Street opposite the Depository building. When asked by David Belin where the shots appeared to have come from, he testified "they appeared to be coming from just west of the Texas School Book Depository." Victoria Adams was north of where Fischer stood, but was high above the motorcade on the fourth floor of the Depository, standing in a fully open window. Three other employees of the Depository standing out in front of the building reported hearing shots which sounded like firecrackers. These witnesses testified that they each heard three shots and the shots appeared to come from west of the Depository. These witnesses were Danny Arce, William Shelley, and Charles Givens. All these witnesses referred to the sounds of the shots as firecracker noises.

Another of the many witnesses present in the plaza who testified to sounds coming from a location other than the Depository was J.W. Foster, a Dallas patrolman stationed as a guard on the Triple Overpass.

Officer Foster testified that he "heard a loud noise, sound like a large firecracker. Kind of dumbfounded me at first, and then I heard the second one. Then the third explosion...."

When asked his opinion as to the source of the shots, Foster testified, "It came from back in toward the corner of Elm and Houston streets."

Diagram 8

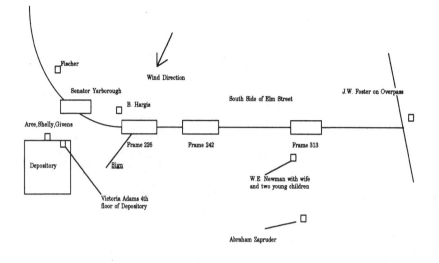

Evidently we can conclude that the testimony of these witnesses may be indicative to determining the location of the shots. Though the testimonies I have reviewed here are in part to their entire accounts, they nevertheless indicated that the shots did not come from the Depository building. If ten men were in the center of a soccer field and only one carried the starter pistol...if three shots were fired and the man who was firing the shots concealed the pistol from view...it would be impossible to determine where the shot actually came from, unless there was evidence to indicate precisely were the shots were fired from. Certainly an open soccer field is somewhat different from Dealey Plaza. When I was in high school and the coach fired the starter gun it was impossible to tell where the shot came from until I located the coach and finding him was still rather hard unless you were standing right next to him when he fired the pistol. Remarkably it, too, sounded like a firecracker noise!

VOLUNTARY STATEMENT. Not Under Arrest. Form No. 86

SHERIFF'S DEPARTMENT
COUNTY OF DALLAS, TEXAS

Before me, the undersigned authority, on this the 22nd day of November A. D. 19 63

personally appeared __Jean Newman__, Address __3893 Clover Lane__
Dallas, Texas

Age __21__, Phone No. __FL 2-4222__

Deposes and says:-

My name is Jean Newman, I live with my parents, my father's name is
G. C. Kimbriel. I work at the Rheem Manufacturing Company.

I was standing right on this side of the Stemmons Freeway sign, about
half-way between the sign and the edge of the building on the corner.
I was by myself, there were other people around watching the motorcade.
The motorcade had just passed me when I heard something that I thought
was a firecracker at first, and the President had just passed me, because
after he had just passed, there was a loud report, it just scared me, and
I noticed that the President jumped, he sort of ducked his head down and
I thought at the time that it probably scared him, too, just like it did
me, because he flinched, like he jumped. I saw him put his elbows like
this, with his hands on his chest.

By this time, the motorcade never did stop, and the President fell to
his left and his wife jumped up on her knees, I believe it was, in the
back of the car on her knees, I couldn't say that for sure. And I
realized then it had been a shot. I looked in the car and she was on
her knees, and he wasn't even visible in the car. I looked around then
and everybody was running every which way, I don't know why I didn't run,
I just stood there and backed up and looked around to see if I could see
anything, but I saw no one whatever with anything that resembled a gun
or anything of that kind.

I just heard two shots. When it happened, I was just looking at the
President and his wife, and when she jumped up in the car, I had my
vision focused on her, and I didn't see anything else, about the others
in the front of the car.

The first impression I had was that the shots came from my right.

Jean Newman

Subscribed and sworn to before me on this the __22nd__ day of __November__ A. D. 19 __63__

rb

James J. Mullady
Notary Public, Dallas County, Texas

Decker Exhibit
Page 1 of 3

VOLUNTARY STATEMENT.   Not Under Arrest.   Form No. 86

SHERIFF'S DEPARTMENT
COUNTY OF DALLAS, TEXAS

Before me, the undersigned authority, on this the <u>22nd</u> day of <u>November</u> A. D. 19<u>63</u>

personally appeared <u>Gayle Newman</u>, Address <u>718 W. Clarendon, Dallas</u>

Age <u>22</u>, Phone No. <u>WH 8-6082</u>

Deposes and says:- My husband, Billy, myself and our children were standing
about halfway between the corner of Elm and Houston and the underpass.
We were the last people in line going toward the underpass. When
President Kennedy's car was about ten feet from us, I heard a noise
that sounded like a firecracker going off. President Kennedy kind of
jumped like he was startled and covered his head with his hands and then
raised up. After I heard the first shot, another shot sounded and Governor
Connally kind of grabbed his chest and lay back on the seat of the car.
When I first saw and heard all of this, I thought it was all of a joke.
Just about the time President Kennedy was right in front of us, I heard
another shot ring out and the President put his hands up to his head.
I saw blood all over the side of his head. About this time Mrs. Kennedy
grabbed the President and he kind of lay over to the side kind of in her
arms. Then my husband, Billy, said it is a shot. We grabbed our two
children and my husband lay on one child and I lay on the other one on
the grass. We started to get up and then all of a sudden we lay back
down. I don't know what it was but another shot may have been fired
that caused us to lay back down. Everyone started running back toward
the brick structure. We got up and went back there. Everyone was saying,
"What happened? What happened.?" Some man from Channel 8 here in Dallas
took us over to the studio where we gave statements of what we had seen.
This is all I saw or know of the incident.

X
X
X
X
X
X
X   *Gayle Newman*

Subscribed and sworn to before me on this the <u>22nd</u> day of <u>November</u> A. D. 19 <u>63</u>

Aleen Davis
Notary Public, Dallas County, Texas

Decker Exhibit
Page 2 of 3

VOLUNTARY STATEMENT.   Not Under Arrest.   Form No. 86

SHERIFF'S DEPARTMENT
COUNTY OF DALLAS, TEXAS

Before me, the undersigned authority, on this the __22nd__ day of __November__ A. D. 19 __63__

personally appeared __William Eugene Newman__, Address __718 W. Clarendon, Dallas, Texas__

Age __22__, Phone No. __WH 8-6082__

Deposes and says:- Today at about 12:45 pm I was standing in a group of people on Elm Street near the west end of the concrete standard when the President's car turned left off Houston Street onto Elm Street. We were standing at the edge of the curb looking at the car as it was coming toward us and all of a sudden there was a noise, apparently gunshot. The President jumped up in his seat, and it looked like what I thought was a firecracker had went off and I thought he had realized it. It was just like an explosion and he was standing up. By this time he was directly in front of us and I was looking directly at him when he was hit in the side of the head. Then he fell back and Governor Connally was holding his middle section. Then we fell down on the grass as it seemed that we were in direct path of fire. It looked like Mrs. Kennedy jumped on top of the President. He kinda fell back and it looked like she was holding him. Then the car sped away and everybody in that area had run upon top of that little mound. I thought the shot had come from the garden directly behind me, that was on an elevation from where I was as I was right on the curb. I do not recall looking toward the Texas School Book Depository. I looked back in the vacinity of the garden.

William E. Newman Jr.

Subscribed and sworn to before me on this the __22nd__ day of __November__ A. D. 19 __63__

G. C. GENTRY

Notary Public, Dallas County, Texas

Decker Exhibit
Page 3 of 3

Gunpowder—An Unanswered Question?

The sixth floor window was approximately sixty-five feet above the motorcade. However the predominant smell of gunpowder lingered on the street below. Earlier reports have suggested that firecrackers were set off in the plaza before the motorcade made its way down Houston Street and turned onto Elm Street where the shooting occurred. However no witnesses testified or recalled the rumor.

With the evidence of the south wind blowing at approximately ten miles an hour, it would appear that the strong smell of the gunpowder reported by Senator Yarborough is conducive to locating the gunman much closer to the presidential motorcade than in a perch stationed nearly two hundred feet above and behind the president. It is inconceivable that the smell of gunpowder could escape from inside the building and be smelled so predominantly on the street below. Where did the shots come from?

W.E. Newman was one of several witnesses who did not testify to the Warren Commission but did give statements to the Dallas police and the FBI. I located Newman's testimony when he appeared in a Tribune Entertainment broadcast of "On Trial—Lee Harvey Oswald." This show aired in 1988 in a live broadcast from Dallas, an event conducted with jurors selected from Dallas County and featuring Gerry Spense as Oswald's defense attorney and Vincent Builiosy as the prosecuting attorney for the government. If Oswald had survived the attack of Jack Ruby, perhaps the witnesses who testified during this eighteen hour event would have instead testified at his trial. Many witnesses testified to things which totally contradict the medical evidence and the eyewitness accounts of witnesses the Commission used to support the "lone assassin—single bullet theory."

Newman reported that he also heard three shots, but his location to the presidential limousine was much closer than the witnesses in front of the Depository and atop the Triple Overpass, several hundred feet either way. Newman's account reflects, too (in my opinion and based on all the related facts in this case), the general concept of not only the source of the shots but the audible decibels of the sounds.

When W.E. Newman heard the first shot, he stated, "We thought at that time, maybe someone had thrown firecrackers or something beside the President's car." He recalled seeing the president raise his hands to his throat, thus indicating that this was indeed a bullet and not a firecracker. Newman's testimony places the *sound* of the shots, in my opinion, in an area next to the president's car; but his testimony to my knowledge never reached the Warren Commission.

Diagram 9

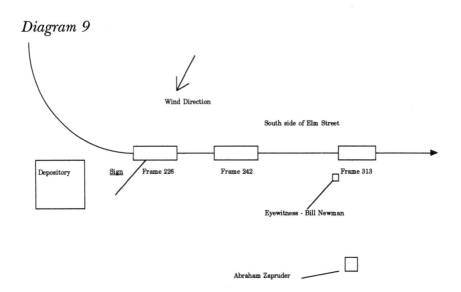

Wind Direction

South side of Elm Street

Depository Sign Frame 226 Frame 242 Frame 313

Eyewitness - Bill Newman

Abraham Zapruder

Newman was approximately forty feet from the presidential limousine when the first shot struck the president. When the third and final shot hit the president in the head, Newman was only eight to twelve feet from the limousine.

Perhaps Newman was too close. He further stated that he thought the third shot came from behind him in the area of the grassy knoll. Other witnesses, such as Charles Brehm who was also standing no less that thirty feet from the car when the shots were fired, did not testify before the Commission.

Jean Newman testified that the first shot hit the president and that he "put his elbows up...like this," indicating the position the president took after being struck by the first shot heard at Frame 226.

Dave Powers, a Kennedy aide, stated, "I had a fleeting impression that the noises appeared to come from the front...."

According to research conducted by Robert Blakey in his book, *Fatal Hour*, Bobby Hargis, a Dallas motorcycle officer, heard the shots and testified, "Well at the time it sounded like the shots were right next to me."

So far as each witness can recall, the *noises* they heard were consistent to the sounds made by firecrackers. If fact each of them thought the first was indeed a firecracker until the president reacted. The location from where each witness stood places the shots in the area immediately west of the Depository. Senator Yarborough, Mrs. Cabell, and Congressman Roberts all detected gunpowder, but where? Where were they when the shots were fired? Where were they when they smelled the gunpowder?

They were in open limousines moving west on Elm Street and their cars slowed but did not stop. What went on in Dallas that was so horrible that the government simply won't tell you?

Exploring a Conspiracy

We know that the Altgens photo was produced to create the illusion of the shots being fired from the Book Depository. A review of the three versions of the Altgens photo shows Mrs. Kennedy's white-gloved hand on the president's forearm while the car is yet behind the Stemmons Freeway sign. We know that Mrs. Kennedy did not place her hand on the president's forearm until Frame 255 of the Zapruder film. At this point in time, two shots had been fired. One hit the Texas governor. The first hit President Kennedy.

Several of the Secret Service men in the photo appear to be looking behind the presidential limousine. Their testimony reflects that they thought they heard a motorcycle backfiring and momentarily turned around to look into the crowd. The effect of the photo alterations provoked the concept of Oswald firing the three shots from above and behind the president, but what really happened? Could they have turned in response to an echo from the high buildings behind them? Are buildings conducive to accepting sound impulses?

Mirror of Doubt will not comfort you with a theory that cannot be proven or substantiated. If you are looking for theories, you have bought the wrong book. The facts of the assassination are public knowledge and together with the evidence and spoken word from that day, they promote conclusions. Are you prepared for a conclusion? A preponderance of evidence is determined by value not by volume. If the evidence is confusing, so must the truth be. The truth of the president's assassination was kept from the public for whatever reason, and although the Commission may never admit to it, it is my opinion, that it knew more than it was willing to let us know.

In previous chapters we spoke about the bullet wounds and the "negatives" experienced by the Warren Commission. These "negatives" which appeared throughout the Report were for the most part withheld from the Official Report, given to President Johnson by the lack of credibility they posed. The gunpowder smell is just one of the many "negatives," as was the backwards motion of the president's head and the credible testimony which contradicts the official version.

We are faced with a serious account of the assassination of our president that for nearly thirty years has wrought controversy and suspicion. When the Warren Commission began its investigation, the facts centered around a rifle found on the sixth floor of the Depository and an eyewitness who later said that he could not positively identify the man in the window as being Lee Harvey Oswald. The further complications of the Commission arose in much of the medical evidence, the testimony of other eyewitnesses, and the government's own re-creation of the event. All too soon facts became theories which could not be proven and may never be.

The wounds sustained by John Connally were medically proven to be caused from one bullet. The bullet entered his back leaving a three centimeter hole and continued on through his chest producing another hole five centimeters in size. The bullet continued on to hit his wrist and although it cannot be substantiated (by the available physical evidence), it struck the interior of the car door and fragmented, sending pieces of the bullet into the limousine windshield and the governor's left knee. Relying on the accuracy of the doctors in Parkland Hospital to have reported a correct size and location of the entry wound in the governor's back, a conclusion can be reached that this bullet was not fired from the Depository. Regardless of the evidence of the rifle and three spent cartridges found on the sixth floor, evidence at this time indicates the presence of two gunmen, simply because the governor's wound of entrance was too low to be caused by a bullet fired from that high. So not only can we conclude that one cartridge case was planted, yet another would appear to have been, given the location and position of the governor when he was struck by the bullet.

The source of the shots indicate that they came from the same direction. There were multiple noises made by a gun not from two directions, but from one, given area which is consistent to the medical truth of this case. The wind direction, too, would have prevented the smell of gunpowder from reaching Elm Street which was south of the knoll.

The smell of gunpowder, the head snap (up, back, and to the left), the initial report of the three millimeter bullet hole in the president's Adam's apple, the wind blowing mildly from the south, the puff of smoke on the grassy knoll where the cigarette butts were found, the autopsy photos released by David Lifton in his book, *Best Evidence*, and many more. These are just a start. Any conclusion reached thirty years ago could have been made only on the basis of facts and evidence on record in the Warren Report examined by its staff.

The evidence of the strong smell of gunpowder, by some law professionals, may not be regarded as evidence at all. If the strong south wind is any indication to determining the location of the smell, it should be examined. It is my opinion that Yarborough could not have been in two places at one time. Just as Oswald could not be in the doorway of the Depository and on the sixth floor of the building at the same time. Therefore it is presumable (in my opinion) that at about the time of the pause between the second and third shots, Yarborough smelled the gunpowder. Where would this place him?

The south wind then carried the smell into the railroad yard behind the grassy knoll where witnesses, whom by David Lifton reports in his book, *Best Evidence*, encountered the smell as well. If Yarborough smelled the gunpowder before witnesses in the railroad yard reported smelling it, there is a variable degree of certainty that Yarborough was closer to the point of origin of the smell than the other witnesses on Houston Street.

Above and Behind

Of the 552 witnesses who either testified or submitted affidavits and statements to the Warren Commission, there were witnesses within twenty feet of the motorcade when the shots were fired who never testified. Nor did the Warren Commission detail the surroundings of the area in the immediate proximity of the limousine when the shots were fired to give those who have never been to Dealey Plaza a mental image of the area.

To the many people who have concluded that thousands of people witnessed the assassination, that concept is a complete exaggeration. The motorcade was nearing the end of its route and had turned onto Elm Street which lead directly to the Stemmons Freeway. The crowd of spectators had thinned by this point, leaving only a few of many thousands who stood waiting to catch a glimpse of the president of the United States. Even those who stood along the west edge of Houston Street hastily moved along the well-kept lawn south of Elm Street to get yet one more look at the motorcade as it left Dallas in route to Trade Mart, where a luncheon was to be held. For many it was truly the first time seeing the president, and tragically it became their last.

Mirror of Doubt has provided its readers with evidence and credible testimony which may be conducive to finding Lee Harvey Oswald innocent of assassinating the president. If the man in the doorway that the Commission refutably recognized as Billy Lovelady was in fact Lee Harvey Oswald, this determination does not preclude the fact that someone else besides Oswald could have been stationed on the sixth floor to complete the diversion; nor does Oswald's presumed innocence lead to a conclusion that he was framed. The events that transpired in Dallas shook the entire world and took the life of your president. Many people who were shed the responsibility of nullifying a conspiracy (in my opinion) performed duties consistent with their titles. However their actions are contemptible to the values this nation was built upon. The responsibility of solving this case and bringing the truth to the sight of the American public is not mine. It rests with the government and the founding principles of justice ensured by the Constitution.

This is truly a great nation and it serves a great people of sacrifice led often astray by misguided beliefs that produce ideals of socialism in a world we strive to retain as a democracy. The great rulers of this nation will not be found in physical form equal to the image of our creator, but in the essence of the freedoms guaranteed by our forefathers, to insure justice, freedom, and truth.

Chapter Seven

The Grand Illusion

The Abraham Zapruder film is without question the most conclusive form of evidence pertaining to the assassination of President John F. Kennedy and has in recent years become once again the center of controversy. Perhaps technology today can transcend the difficulties faced by the Warren Commission thirty years ago, when the details of the film, in 1963, proved to be inconclusive to other findings.

Though examiners of the film claim it can only be interpreted one way; the Commission's general attitude was that its detail did not establish the presence of another gunman. It regarded the fatal wound which the president suffered as the result of a rear entry missile, in part to the medical autopsy examination conducted at Bethesda Naval Hospital. The film is perhaps the only evidence which would substantiate the contradictions of the official version. Was it possible for Kennedy to be shot from behind based on what we witness in the film?

When the Warren Commission concluded that it wasn't necessary to determine which shot struck Governor Connally, it made a grave error in judgment. If the film details the governor reacting to the bullet that struck him, it would answer many of the questions that have remained unanswered over the past thirty years. The significance of determining which of the first two shots hit Governor Connally, too, would settle the long disputed theory of the single bullet which was supposed to have struck both men. Another value would determine if in fact a gunman was not able to fire the second shot in the time allowable. The probability of a second gunman could then be established based on a trajectory study of the wounds.

We know that the gunman on the sixth floor could not have been Lee Harvey Oswald if he was standing in the doorway of the Depository as the shot rang out. Realizing that this does not preclude the fact that a gunman or someone was seen by witnesses in the window both before and after the shots were fired, it does however raise the question, why was the Warren

Commission convinced of Lee Harvey Oswald's guilt? In previous chapters we have examined this question, but to resolve it we must look deeper into *Mirror of Doubt* for that answer.

When I first determined John Connally's position when he was struck by a second bullet, that determination caused me to conclude that both the Commission and Governor Connally were wrong. The Commission was wrong about the "single bullet theory" and John Connally was wrong about facing left center. What does this mean? It means that a second gunman in Dealey Plaza is detectable! Two shooters or if the Commission was right about the first bullet hitting the president from behind, possibly three. Yet John Connally only suffered from one gunshot wound, indicating that Dr. Perry was correct about the first bullet striking the president from the front.

In examination of the trajectory analysis study offered by the FBI in its reenactment of the assassination, we determined that it may not have been possible for the bullet to strike the president in his back and exit at a location higher on the front of his throat. The analysis showed that a 20.11 degree downward angle of this bullet and the position of the president at the time would have precluded the possibility of these wounds being connected. Also if no other wounds were found by the examining pathologists during the autopsy, Dr. Malcolm Perry can be given a high degree of credibility to his reporting an entrance wound in the President's Adam's apple.

Gunpowder on the Street Below

We know that a strong smell of gunpowder was evident on the plaza grounds in the area of the motorcade route. The south wind present in Dealey Plaza dissipated this smell towards the grassy knoll area where as the odor was nevertheless apparent, it was less predominant. This smell in the area of the railroad yard led many people to conclude that a gunman was present somewhere on the knoll. However the evidence of the south wind takes us back to Elm Street and the Zapruder film to a possible origin. Since Senator Yarborough would have been the first eyewitness to report smelling the gunpowder and with the evidence of the south wind, perhaps the area south of Elm Street would be an accurate place to begin. If the shots were fired from the knoll, the south wind would have prevented the gunpowder smell from reaching the area in proximity to Senator Yarborough, Mrs. Cabell and Congressman Roberts, all of whom smelled gunpowder from open-top limousines.

An aerial photo of Dealey Plaza showing Elm and Houston Streets gives us a bird's-eye view of the assassination area and a general visual structure for the scene of the event. The plaza is an open-spaced area which has similar qualities to a city park, yet it has no fireplaces or tables that allow access to the public for picnic lunches. Elm Street, which leads to Stemmons Freeway, intersects Houston Street at the southeast corner of the Depository building. As the motorcade turns off Houston Street onto Elm, the Texas School Book Depository is located to the right of the president. Three shots are heard and the majority of the witnesses testify that the sounds of the shots did not appear to come from the Depository building where the rifle was found.

Critical Moments—A Documentary Analysis

The assassination was a well-planned, carefully-orchestrated conspiracy. Furthermore it worked. The assassin took the president's life while people watched in horror and achieved the goal of getting away. If the implications of the Zapruder film and the other evidence have substantial weight, the conclusions you draw will be shared by many other readers. During this analysis we will converge on the style of the assassination and the premeditated act of vengeance that ultimately took the life of this nation's president. What happened in Dealey Plaza?

Frame 222 will begin the sequence of frames that I have often, in my research, referred to as the first critical moment. In total there are three critical moments. Frames 222 to 230 will be analyzed as the first, Frames 231 to 265 the second, and the remainder beginning with Frame 266 to the end as the third. In Frame 222 we see Governor Connally has emerged from behind the Stemmons Freeway sign. He is facing towards the right looking at the crowd of spectators and has been since Frame 160 prior to the car entering behind the sign. Agent Roy Kellerman, seated in front of Governor Connally, appears to be looking to his right as well.

The crowd, although not visible in the Zapruder film, is very scant. There is an estimated twenty-five people on the north side of Elm Street and about dozen or so remaining on the south side of the street. A view of the south side shows two men in the right-hand margin of the frame. The Warren Commission would have you believe there were thousands of people who witnessed the assassination. This was not so.

The First Critical Moment

Governor Connally in Frame 223 appears to be holding a carnation or bluish object slightly out in front of his chest. This object, which will be seen throughout the entire Zapruder film, will be mentioned as it appears. Though it isn't quite clear what the governor is doing, it is safe to concur that he is looking into the crowd of spectators standing on the curb, as he indicated in testimony. (See photo composite of Frame 225/223.)

Frame 223 exposes Mrs. Kennedy in full view of the camera, yet Connally obstructs full view of the president's wife. It can be noted that Mrs. Kennedy does not have her hand on the president's forearm at this time and will not until Frame 255. The object is still visible (slightly higher at about shoulder height) and it is unclear if Connally has seen the president or if any shots have been fired. Agent Kellerman is still focused to the right.

For practical purposes Frame 224 will be skipped.

In Frame 225 both the president and Governor Connally are visible by the lens of the Zapruder camera. The bright sunlight cast a reflection and the faces of both men are shadowed on the right. The president appears to be alarmed by something and is looking towards the front and slightly to the right. He raises his right hand just as he appears from behind the sign. Perhaps he has noticed something or is just beginning to react to a bullet strike. The governor now, is facing slightly more towards the right-center and Kellerman still looks on.

According to the FBI, President Kennedy's reaction to the first bullet strike is barely apparent in this frame. Close examination of the film, however, reveals that while his right hand is raised, he has not completely shown any sign of the bullet entering his body.

In Frame 226 the president clearly reacts (as the FBI reported) to the first bullet fired in Dealey Plaza as his right hand (which was raised slightly in Frame 225) is pulled quickly to his throat and is soon accompanied by his left hand. His face painfully shows signs that he has been struck. The President of the United States has been shot and the bullet has severed his windpipe. Governor Connally does not appear to be affected by this first bullet and regarded in his testimony that he heard this shot and it appeared to come from over his right shoulder. The velocity of the bullet would have made it clear that by the time the sound was heard, the bullet had hit its mark. Therefore it is safe to conclude that the president was not struck until Frame 226 but may have heard the sound of the shot at Frame 225.

Since the preponderance of evidence suggested that only three shots were heard, this was the first shot fired and it hit President Kennedy. What needs to be determined is why this bullet did or did not hit John Connally, seated directly in front of the president. (See Commission's Exhibit #895, view through rifle scope.)

Frame 224
President Kennedy having not been struck by the first bullet fired begins to react.

Frame 225
The president's reactions to the first bullet fired are barely apparent in this frame. His right hand is raised slightly.

Frame 226
The president clearly reacts to a bullet traveling at a rate of 1800 feet per second. This bullet should continue on to strike John Connally seated in front of the president in the very next frame, as the Zapruder camera recorded the shots at eighteen frames per second.

If the Warren Commission's infamous "single bullet theory" is correct, we can determine in the very next frames that this same bullet (which has caused the president to reach for his throat) should have continued on and struck John Connally.

From reviewing John Connally's positions and testimony we recall that he heard the first shot and turned to his right to see if he could catch the president out of the corner of his eye. We see that he is facing to the right prior to the bullet striking the president. In testimony Governor Connally gave the impression that he was facing forward when he heard this shot.

We can expect from the remaining frames in this first critical moment series of the Zapruder film for Governor Connally to have time to turn to the right, not see the president, and then turn to the left and be struck by a second bullet, but only if his account is truthful will he be facing forward at the time.

The president now is reacting in Frame 226 and the bullet has pierced his throat. We can now presume that this bullet will continue on in a downward thrust (at the designated 20.11 degree angle) to strike John Connally and substantiate the Commission's ruling of the president being struck from behind, by a single bullet.

On the basis of the evidence that initially came from Parkland Hospital of an entrance wound being located in the president's Adam's apple, we can determine the trajectory (by disregarding Dr. Perry's account) and draw a mental line to the point of entrance in Governor Connally's back. When the Warren Commission examined the film, its conclusion, based on FBI re-enactment of these frames, that this first bullet hit both men and was fired from behind. The trajectory analysis study conducted by the FBI indicated that by the view through the rifle scope, the bullet will continue on to strike the governor his left side. (See FBI reenactment of Frame 225.)

If Governor Connally had heard this shot as he reported in his testimony and in lieu of the fact the president has clearly reacted, the governor should at this point in the Zapruder film (Frame 227) be turning in response to the right. A review of the film will indicate only the "juggling act" he performs with his Stetson hat as the president reacts to the first bullet fired in Dallas.

When examining the Zapruder film, we must be aware that it recorded the assassination of the president at eighteen frames per second. This means that for every second in time (one thousand one), the movie camera takes 18 still-shot motion pictures. Ballistic studies conducted by the FBI indicated that the bullet traveled at a rate of 1800 feet per second. So for every single frame of the Zapruder film we can expect the bullet to travel one hundred feet. If Kennedy is struck at Frame 226, John Connally should show signs of being hit at Frame 227.

Simply the governor should show reaction to the bullet now!

135

Within Frames 227 to 230, the president continues to react to the first shot fired. As we recall the president began his initial reactions to the first shot by raising his right hand in Frame 225 with the palm of his hand facing slightly outward, though it is not quite apparent in Frame 225. This reactive motion was followed first by his right hand and then by his left. These frames lead to a point where in Frame 230, the president has given every indication as to being shot. His left hand is positioned under his chin and his right hand slightly higher, blocking partial view of his lower face. In this frame there is no question that the president, beginning at Frame 226, is reacting to a bullet wound.

Governor Connally stated in testimony before the Warren Commission, "After hearing the sound of the shot, determined that it had already struck its mark." Too, the governor was nearly the only witness to relate the sound of this shot as a rifle shot. Other witnesses reported hearing firecrackers or motorcycles backfiring. The location or source of the shots according to eyewitness testimony, was west of the Depository. (re: Victoria Adams) If this were true and this shot did not hit Connally seated directly in front of Kennedy as the Warren Commission stated it did, the accountability for this bullet is yet to be determined. It did not hit the governor and was not found in the car.

In Frame 226 the governor is facing more to the left than he appeared in the previous Frame 225, when the president first shows signs of reacting to the first shot. Following the reactions of Governor Connally to the bullet sound (while facing right center as the president reacts), the governor turns to his left to a point where he is facing center in Frame 230. So here in regard to a single, first bullet striking both men, we have President Kennedy reacting more and more to a bullet strike and John Connally reacting less and less. (re: Frames 222-230)

Frame 228
Connally shows no sign of being struck by the bullet which has clearly passed through the president via the Adam's apple.

Frame 229
As the president reacts more and more, the Texas governor reacts less and less, and the wrist is nowhere near the chest exit wound.

Frame 230
The wrist, which has clearly been turned inward, holds the Stetson hat firmly. One bullet caused the wounds sustained by John Connally, yet the Warren Commission ruled that the first bullet that struck the president also hit the governor.

John Connally, who testified in the hearings conducted by the Commission, reported that after he heard the shot he turned to his right to try to catch the president in the corner of his eye. The president reacts to the bullet in Frame 225 and is unharmed prior to this frame, in the preceding frames of 222 to 224. Why is it that the Commission did not determine from the film that Connally did not turn to the right in response to the first shot as he said he did? He turns only to the left and we see no sign of this right turn he offered as testimony.

This is a critical moment of the assassination which needs to be addressed. To raise a question, if Governor Connally did not turn in response to the first shot as he said he did, could the first bullet have come from behind? Could the governor have actually been turning in response to a shot which came from the front?

In Frames 228, 229, and 230, the governor's posture is such that the medical evidence clearly substantiates the claim that the governor has not been struck by the first bullet. Notice first the Stetson hat held in his right hand at Frame 230. As the president began reacting to the bullet in Frame 225, Governor Connally appeared to reach over towards his left, grabbing his Stetson hat with his right hand. This would be an impossible feat if a bullet were to strike the radius bone in his wrist. The hat is raised up, across in front of him whereby in Frames 228 to 230, it is held by his right hand and it is brought down from above shoulder height. The constant movement of his wrist (as seen in the film) simply does not allow a bullet to strike the wrist after exiting the president's throat. As aforementioned, at no time during this sequence or prior to Frame 242; (as we'll learn) does Governor Connally's wrist align with the point in his chest that the bullet exited.

In Frame 230 the hat is clearly held in his right hand and his wrist is unharmed. If the medical evidence stands, we must conclude that the bullet which struck President Kennedy came from the front, for two reasons: (1) the governor's smooth reach for his Stetson hat clarifies this perception, and (2) Connally shows no sign of being hit.

The problem with this critical moment is that both the Warren Commission and Governor Connally were mistaken about the event. Where the Commission, by the promoting the "single bullet theory" of the FBI, concluded that either the first or second bullet missed both men, it also concluded that one bullet caused the wounds of Governor Connally after it exited the President's throat. The basis of this conclusion is that John Connally was in front of the president, where after the bullet exited, it continued on to hit the only object in front of the president. This initial finding was conducive to a shot which did not come from the front, according to the Commission.

The Commission's theory cannot be accepted on the basis of the Zapruder film. If the first bullet hit only the president, as eyewitness reports indicated, the second bullet did not. It did, however, hit the governor.

Remember only three shots were heard and the Zapruder film is the hard evidence which your government should have used to determine Oswald's sole guilt.

The truth?

Governor Connally's recollection of the assassination attempt was vague, in that his story not only changed from his first reports, but the account in question does not reflect his actions in the Zapruder film. In viewing Frames 222 to 230 we cannot credit the testimony of Governor Connally as reflecting the truth. If he had turned to his right in an attempt to see the president after he heard the sound of the first shot, we would see it in the Zapruder frames! We do not. Only the president's reactions to a bullet strike are visible in Frames 225 to 230. Therefore Governor Connally was right about not being hit by the first bullet but was mistakenly inaccurate about his motivation and actions when hearing the sound of the first shot. Could he also have mistaken the sound as an echo from the buildings above and behind the motorcade? Or did the medical evidence establish a trajectory which prevented this?

What was the trajectory established by the autopsy photos concerning the president's throat wound? How does the Commission regard what appears to be a wound at the base of the president's hairline which Dr. Humes and Dr. Boswell (the examining pathologists at Bethesda Naval Hospital) failed to disclose in the official autopsy report?

While the first wound sustained by President Kennedy has always been controversial, Dr. Malcolm Perry, we can recall, reported seeing a three millimeter wound just below the Adam's apple. Yet in order to strengthen the president's chances for survival, Perry performed a tracheotomy incision over the wound. This completely obliterated any evidence of a front entry wound in the president's throat and Dr. Perry was reported to have been mistaken by the Warren Commission. It is fair to assume that if the governor was not hit by this bullet, it did not come from the rear, high above the motorcade from a sixth floor window.

The smell of gunpowder, too, must be credited, since the witnesses who reported smelling the odor linked it to the sound of the shots (re: Senator Ralph Yarborough). Only seconds passed from the time the shots sounded to the time the reports of the smell were noted. The Commission placed the smell of gunpowder in the "negative file." *Mirror of Doubt* places it in the "evidence pile" with the credible testimony of the witness who heard the shots being fired at the president.

It is possible that the first shot could have come from the knoll, but is it also possible that a true bullet path has been established by the autopsy? If the wound at the base of the hairline is consistent with being related to the throat wound reported by Dr. Malcolm Perry; can a probable trajectory be established on these superficial facts alone?

The Shooting of a Texas Governor

The second critical moment in Dallas centers on the bullet wound sustained by Governor Connally. Certainly a game of chicken wasn't being played in Dallas, yet the shooting of John Connally created problems for the Warren Commission, the FBI, and the first gunman. Doctors in Parkland Hospital and autopsy surgeons from Bethesda Naval Hospital reported that the wound which transited the windpipe of the president would not have been fatal and the president would have survived this assassination attempt. It is apparent by the shooting of Governor Connally that the first gunman was required to fire yet a second shot at President Kennedy.

The results that stem from the initial wound sustained by the president created a chain of tragic sparks and controversy surrounding a second gunshot and the president's fatal head wound by yet a third.

Notably the Zapruder film retains the responsible conclusion for determining the sequence of frames which disclose the reactions of Governor Connally as the bullet passes through his body. In Frame 231 we see Governor Connally still facing forward and the president still grasping at his throat (perhaps in an effort to relieve the tension being placed on his throat injury after the bullet passed). Noting that by Frame 227, Mrs. Kennedy is sure that her husband has sustained a gunshot wound. She is deeply alarmed and afraid for his safety.

In Frames 224 to 231 she can be seen looking towards her husband. Roy Kellerman, who testified to hearing the first shot, remains facing to the right of the limousine and provides no indication that any shots have been fired. Suddenly in the next frames of this critical sequence a second shot rings out in Dealey Plaza striking Governor Connally, but not before he has turned completely to his right facing the car door, away from the Depository.

Another interesting aspect of the second critical moment is the reaction that we are expected to see from Roy Kellerman, the Secret Service agent seated in front of John Connally.

In testimony this agent reported also turning to his right. Kellerman reported, too, that he saw the president and heard him say, "Oh God I'm hit." We can only wonder why his testimony will remain inconsistent with his actions captured on the Zapruder film.

In Frames 232 to 240, Governor Connally begins his turn. His left hand comes up from out of sight and joins his right hand on the Stetson hat while he is completing his turn to the right. In this turn he can be seen wording, "Oh, no, no, no," a statement his wife, Nellie, testified hearing before the Warren Commission. In this turn the president's wife continues to look at her husband in bewilderment. The governor is unharmed thus far, but is turning in an attempt to see the president. Mrs. Connally recalled that after she heard "Oh, no, no, no," a second loud, frightening noise sounded, and she saw her husband recoil to the right.

If Mrs. Connally's testimony can be regarded as accurate, we can expect Governor Connally to first react in a left thrust motion to the bullet that struck him in the back, as this must occur before he recoils from the shot. This would also be a clear indication of a second shot striking only the governor.

Mrs. Kennedy is unsure, it seems why the governor is turning in response (in these frames) and is concerned for the future safety of her husband. As Frame 238 begins, Mrs. Kennedy looks at Governor Connally. Agent Kellerman, apparently unaware that anything at all has happened, remains focused to the right. Mrs. Connally only looks towards the governor. Perhaps Mrs. Kennedy has realized that the governor has not been hit. Governor Connally heard the first shot, as did Mrs. Connally.

Without a doubt in Frames 241 to 243, we see Governor Connally reacting to a bullet that enters his back. This bullet then exits his chest below the right nipple and crashes through the wrist of his right hand.

The conclusive evidence that Frame 243 establishes is by the reaction of the pinky finger on the right hand of Governor Connally as the bullet strikes the radius bone in his wrist. The wrist, once horizontal in Frame 241, can be seen visibly turned downward as the bullet makes contact, causing the cartilage connected to the pinky finger to be severed.

Frame 241
Now nearly two seconds after the president reacts, Governor Connally, facing the car door, reacts. Note the Depository is behind the motorcade.

Frame 242
The bullet enters the governor in the back below the shoulder blade and begins its track through the chest. The wrist which sustained damage first on its backside, is nearly horizontal but in line with the chest exit wound.

Frame 243
As the bullet makes contact with the governor's wrist, the wrist no longer remains in a horizontal position. The wrist is turned immediately downward by the bullet's impact and the bones and cartilege are now damaged causing his pinky finger to protrude sightly as the bullet strikes his wrist.

The evidence of the bullet striking Governor Connally within these frames suggests that the location of the unknown gunman was a point to the southwest of the Depository, perhaps a distance away from the motorcade. The position of Governor Connally at the time the bullet strikes his wrist can be seen in the photographic still-frame viewing of the Zapruder film.

This conclusion was not reached by the Commission though the wrist being part of an extremity, shows clear sign of reaction. We must also conclude that by close examination of the Zapruder film, that at no time during the film does the governor's wrist come into alignment with his chest exit wound until Frame 241 of the Zapruder film.

The Limousine Windshield

In the remaining frames of this second critical sequence, Agent Kellerman continues looking towards the right on the north side of Elm Street. If the implications of the Zapruder film provide us with a concise analysis of this event, even more questions remain. Here two shots have been fired causing the witnesses along the banks of Elm Street to turn in response to the firecracker-sounding gunfire. What about Roy Kellerman, a trained Secret Service agent? This guy doesn't budge! In fact he remains turned to the right from Frames 160 to 250 at a point in time that even the official version notes that two shots have been fired.

The reactions of Agent Roy Kellerman in the Zapruder film do not substantiate or verify the claims of his testimony before the Warren Commission. In the Zapruder film, Kellerman remains looking to the right from Frames 222 to 245 where he begins to turn in response to what may be a bullet fragmenting, striking the limousine windshield after hitting the car door. Commission Exhibit #350 shows a picture of the broken windshield taken by the FBI. The Warren Commission, as it did to many important aspects of this case, failed to conclude which shot struck the windshield.

Commission Exhibit #350

The limousine windshield was broken from the inside, but the Warren Commission failed to determine which bullet caused the damage. The Commission also stated it could not determine which bullet struck Governor Connally. If it had examined the Zapruder film with serious interest, it would have determined that the second shot struck Connally and continued on to strike the windshield, drawing the attention of both Greer and Kellerman, who ducked down as a result.

The governor's wrist in Frame 243 when the bullet made contact would have prevented the bullet from exiting the car. Therefore is it also possible that the car door sustained damage which might have ricocheted the bullet into the windshield? The other bullets were found to not have caused this damage. (Photo courtesy of Assassination Archives and Research Center.)

The actions of Agent Kellerman have always puzzled me. Two shots have been fired from Frames 222 to 243 and Agent Kellerman testified before the Warren Commission that when he heard the first noise, he turned to his right, looked over his shoulder, and saw the president had slumped, raising his hands to his throat.

Kellerman also testified, "I heard him say Oh God I am hit." (referring to the president). Yet President Kennedy had sustained a wound to his throat. Medically speaking, was it possible for the president to even speak after the bullet passed into his throat? I doubt it. Nevertheless Kellerman could not have seen the president slump, because he didn't turn around until after the second shot had been fired. The fact that Kellerman testified to hearing the president speak sparked controversy for both the FBI and the Warren Commission. Secret Service Agent Clint Hill ran immediately to the car after hearing the first shot and yet another dove immediately on top of Lyndon Johnson, Agent Kellerman looks on. He sees nothing and reacts only to the bullet striking the windshield. This same officer reported hearing a flurry of shots after the third shot struck the president in the head.

The significance of when Kellerman reacted to the gunshots is relevant, in both how he reacted and under what circumstances he reacted to determining which bullet struck the limousine windshield. (Consequently Agent Greer also turned simultaneously to Agent Kellerman.) What drew their attention? The sound of the shots certainly didn't cause Kellerman to turn. What about Greer?

Though it remains only plausible that the second shot struck the windshield, it is a consistent solution to the position of John Connally's wrist when it is struck by the bullet in Frame 243. Close examination of the frame shows his wrist below the alignment of the top of the car door. The FBI reported that no part of the car was struck by fragments other than the windshield which was *broken from the inside.*

This bullet striking the governor's wrist where it did could not have exited the car prior to fragmenting, thus sending a piece of the bullet into Connally's left thigh. The only photograph showing the inside of the car door released by the Commission or the FBI has been cropped, making it impossible to further substantiate this claim. Common sense says that if the governor appears to be hit while in this position, the bullet would have struck the car door and subsequently fragmented sending pieces into the windshield and causing Greer and Kellerman to turn simultaneously.

In Frame 255 Mrs. Kennedy, in an attempt to prevent further harm from coming to her husband, reacts the way any president's wife should act. She places her hand on his forearm and begins to comfort him. As the bullet enters the governor's back, his shoulder buckles and his entire facial expression changes. His open mouth in the subsequent frames from 243 indicate that the pain is clearly evident and becomes even moreso after the bullet makes contact with his wrist.

The evidence of the wrist being smacked by the bullet in Frame 243 is clearly indicative of a gunman located behind Connally, not in the sixth floor window of the Depository to his right. The limousine window behind Mrs. Connally is rolled up approximately ten inches.

The Third Critical Moment

In the third and final critical moment in the attempt to take the life of President Kennedy, thus removing him from office, we find more of the "negatives" experienced by the Commission. This sequence of events begins with Frame 266 of the Zapruder film. It is apparent by the reactions of both William Greer and Roy Kellerman that both men are now well aware of bullets striking the people in the car.

Governor Connally, now looking into the back seat, can be seen effected from the bullet entering his back. The wrist and his right hand are now held draped over his left forearm and we can expect him to simply leave his wounded wrist lying carefully where it is. The shattered appearance of the wrist can be seen drooped over the left forearm with his fingers spread apart. (Frame 289)

In the remaining frames prior to the sequence of this third critical moment, we'll begin with Frame 311 of the Zapruder film. Frames 312 and 313 show explicit detail of the bullet contacting the president's head a fraction of a second before the contact becomes apparent. In this sequence Governor Connally, seated in front of the president is in an upright position, looking into the back seat both at Mrs. Kennedy and the president. Mrs. Kennedy, terrified for her husband's safety, looks intensely at Governor Connally but says nothing, fully aware that both men have been seriously wounded

This particular part of the assassination attempt of President Kennedy has always puzzled me in that shots are presumably being fired into the car, yet the reactions of the people being fired at are not consistent, in my opinion, to what these people should be doing. It is apparent in these frames that John Connally, while sitting up, looks into the back seat at the president and his wife, Jackie. The impression I get is that the governor wants to see how badly the president is hurt and holds the disposition that the shooting has stopped. With Jackie, it is apparent only after the fatal head shot that rockets the president's head in a violent backwards motion which causes her to flee from the car.

It seems to me that if bullets were being fired from an unknown location into a presidential limousine, the passengers of the car would duck down. As we watch the Zapruder film, the opposite is true.

While the president has been seriously wounded by what Dr. Malcolm Perry initially reported as an entrance wound in the president's Adam's apple and Governor Connally has been struck by a separate bullet below the shoulder blade, Mrs. Kennedy is fearful for her husband's life. After yet another attempt is taken to successfully remove the president from office, she flees from the car. This is not only unusual, it is puzzling. Governor Connally, on the other hand, is a noted hunter. After what he reported to the Commission was a shot coming from behind the motorcade and having sustained a bullet wound, he makes no attempt to save his wife from harm. What about Nellie? Does she get down out of the line of fire? Is there any immediate response by any member riding in the presidential limousine?

The driver, William Greer, as he turns to look into the back seat unconsciously removes pressure from the accelerator. A bullet has struck the windshield and the vehicle in turn slows. As the third shot is fired, an instant before the bullet strikes the president in the head, the driver touches his brake. When the bullet does make contact with the president, Will Greer is looking directly into the back seat at President Kennedy. He then turns simultaneously, stepping on the accelerator.

In the final frames, as the blood and cerebral fluid become apparent, further substantiating facts can be found. Though it does not become evidence until it is submitted, the Warren Commission was not able to detect what we are about to witness.

Frame 311
No damage has been inflicted by the fatal shot which effectively removed the president from the Oval Office.

Frame 312
The flash reported by a witness prior to the visibility of blood and cerebral fluid.

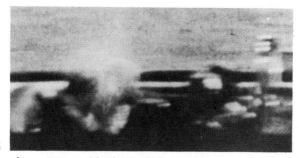

Frame 313
The bullet makes contact with the president causing his head to be propelled violently backwards by the impact of this shot. Note that no damage has been inflicted on the rear of the head and the downward separation of blood and cerebral fluid.

Technology Today

In any still-frame enlargement of Frame 312 released since 1963, I have not witnessed what appears to be a flash in front of Mrs. Kennedy's face prior to the bullet inflicting damage to the president's head. I have examined this frame under the pretense of the shots coming from behind, as well as from the front. In both studies I was convinced that the bullet does not contact the president's head in Frame 312, but it is very close. In this frame the flash is apparent in that it tends to light up in three-dimensional form the area in front of Mrs. Kennedy's face and continues in an upwards, yet backwards spray—over the top of the president's head. The appearance of this flash prior to the bullet coming into contact with the president's head is conducive to a bullet wound inflicting damage by a shot that could have only come from the front. The white flash is visible prior to the blood and cerebral fluid becoming visible, one eighteenth of a second before Frame 313. There are no double images displayed in this frame.

Frame 313 and the following frames show both the bullet contacting the president's head and the violent backwards motion as the bullet makes contact. In Frame 313, to further substantiate the flash where it was visible in Frame 312, it is not visible in Frame 313 or Frame 311. This is conclusive proof that it appeared before the bullet makes contact, in lieu of the fact that it disappears when the bullet contacts the president's head. Examination of these frames has provided a basis for determining the probable location of a gunman which in recent years has been suggested to be on the grassy knoll. Frame 312, however, shows the flash extending over the top of the president's head as it appears in a bright glow in front of Mrs. Kennedy's face. The appearance of the flash on the Zapruder film may, by advanced technology, be examined in order to determine its relevancy to the fatal head shot. If it can be detected elsewhere in the photographic evidence, perhaps the mystery of the president's death will not remain much longer. This flash is not apparent in Frame 311.

In the remaining frames of the Zapruder film, we have marked the notable actions of Mrs. Kennedy as she flees from the car. The president has clearly been fatally shot and Governor Connally, instantaneous to the shot striking the president's head, rolls over onto his left side.

Can You Solve the J.F.K. Conspiracy?

Can we reach a conclusion based on the facts we have examined so far? It may be possible to draw conclusions based on facts, substantiated evidence, credible testimony, and the Warren Commission's exhibits, but is it the responsibility of the people of a democracy to draw conclusions? Everyone at one time or another has commented on the legal system used by our country. Some regard it as corporate while others unfair. Our legal system was designed with the intention of functioning as a free and independent representative of truth, on the basis of the integrity it possesses. If the facts in this case are clear, they speak alone.

We have spoken about the truth and have read how a noted philosopher regarded the truth as being "quite beyond the reach of satire." One can mock a wild guess, but the truth is acquired by sticking to the facts and hard evidence. If we can protect our democratic form of government, then surely we can use its foundation to procure justice to render the truth in a world now unsettled by doubt and frustration. It was not the intent of our founding fathers that crimes against the people receive no punishment. Life, liberty, and property are the three basic elements of freedom, all of which can not be construed to deny or disparage the rights of others. Our Constitution is clear.

When the facts of the assassination first became known to me and I realized that the Warren Commission had failed to adequately analyze the event, it was also clear that the same areas of concern the Commission had thirty years ago were also mine. If the Warren Commission did not aid in a cover-up conspiracy, what prevented it from viewing the information as we have here in *Mirror of Doubt* and reach a possible conclusion that two gunmen were present in Dealey Plaza, of which neither was Lee Harvey Oswald?

Certainly the task of the Warren Commission was not an impossible feat and the number of reasons for the dismissal of the "negatives," which have proven to be "positives" would be limited. The Warren Commission had a goal and I prefer to think that of the four possible scenarios which justify what happened in Dallas, the first is true and all that remain are mere unaccountable suppositions. Nevertheless nearly thirty years have gone by and the only government investigation after the Warren Commission concluded that Oswald acted alone was the House Select Committee on Assassinations and that was fourteen years ago! The possibilities are limited. What happened?

1. The Warren Commission and the FBI could not substantiate their suspicions and simply did not receive enough information or have the resources available to gather a preponderance of evidence. The Commission then would have secretly concluded that there was perhaps another assassin, but since a preestablished line of prosecution had been established by the FBI it needed to safeguard the facts and serve Oswald as the lone assassin for a temporary solution. It continued to investigate allegations of a conspiracy but has still failed to come up with a solution to the event. Any evidence that would have created

suspicion in the minds of the researchers and concerned citizens was then subsequently locked away in a secret file.

2. The Commission members conceded to the intimidation efforts of government officials willing to cover the truth (re: Lyndon Johnson), but regarded the integrity of the nation and made a vain attempt in passing the information to the public in a manner that would not be questioned. (Some of this is contained in the twenty-six-volume set.) This would have made cowards out of the Commission members, unless these same efforts were linked to the above possibility and we have seen no sign of a continued investigation other than independent researchers for the past thirty years.

3. The Commission concluded beyond a reasonable doubt that Oswald fired all three shots and no conspiracy of any kind existed. Therefore, the "negatives" would only have related to David Ferrie and other associates of Oswald and Ruby. The gunpowder would then have meant nothing and the evidence of the head snap and all the other relevant information and credible testimony was simply inconclusive. With the FBI handling the case, what more could the Commission members prove? They played golf and made as many meetings as they could, but relinquished authority given to them by an executive order to other government agencies involved in investigating the assassination.

4. The assassination attempt failed and the autopsy photos were altered to create the illusion of the president's death to a lone assassin firing from the southeast corner on the sixth floor of the Depository. Since the only way to safeguard and provide security to the living President would be to stage his death, they forged the autopsy documents and provided only eyewitnesses who threatened the security of this covert operation access to John Kennedy. With no rear entry wounds reported on the body from Parkland Hospital and the Bethesda officials not having seen the president's body since it never left Dallas, these people, too, were required to partake in this cover-up conspiracy. The president survived and since no criminal charges could be lodged against the suspected criminal for the president's murder, it became necessary to completely destroy all evidence linking the assassin to another location in Dealey Plaza. With John Connally shot, the president only wounded, and Jackie unharmed, the nation had mourned the death of the president and it became history that could never be recovered.

A close friend of mine holds the position of justice of the peace. When I spoke to him about the facts that I had obtained regarding the assassination of President Kennedy, he confirmed my suspicions. What I shared with him wasn't anything different than the facts we have reviewed in *Mirror of Doubt*. Indeed if the opposite were true from the Warren Commission's conclusion that the shots struck the president from behind, would it not also preclude the theory of a gunman being located on the grassy knoll? I reenacted the position of President Kennedy when the bullet struck him in the head during my discussion with my friend and his reply was startling. Our discussion ended soon after and he told me he would like to read *Mirror of Doubt* when it was finished. The response I got from my friend, the judge, was indicative of many other responses I have received throughout my researching of the assassination of President John F. Kennedy while reviewing the enhanced Archives's version of the Zapruder film with them in slow motion.

On several occasions I have conducted various viewings of the Zapruder film with close friends, who soon became associate references in my efforts to bring to you *Mirror of Doubt*. Twelve out of twelve people who watched the film with me as I explained the related facts about the smell of gunpowder and the flash or glow that appears prior to the visibility of the blood and cerebral fluid concurred the third shot fired in Dealey Plaza came from the front. The position of Governor Connally and his wrist being smacked so hard by the bullet that it is torn from his Stetson hat provide the location of a gunman south of the Depository. The evidence of the head snap, the smell of gunpowder, and the flash caused responses that stifled me, but I too was convinced that the government of the United States, my government, should reopen the investigation.

It seems like the right thing to do. We can only hope.

During much of my research I felt uncomfortable. I knew I was about as close as any one person working alone on this case would want to be and I didn't want to just forget it. I suppose that in the initial stages of my work, I hoped that the media would just disclose the information but soon realized it wasn't its responsibility. I had commissioned myself to resolving the controversy surrounding the president's death and I had most all the facts. Those I don't have, our government has.

All too soon it became apparent to me that other researchers had a preconceived notion that the smell of gunpowder was indicative of locating President Kennedy's assassin. In 1986 when I saw the Zapruder film for the first time, I knew he was shot from the front. I can't tell you how I knew, but I did. I've known about the smell of gunpowder since the 1970s, when a relative of mine gave me the 23 November, 1963 issue of the *New York Daily News*, but have not until now obtained the resources sufficient enough to produce *Mirror of Doubt*.

The preference of researchers in the past has been to release the information to the public in such a way that any interested would focus cautiously on the facts. I agree this must be done. One example is that one researcher noted the wind direction in Dealey Plaza came from the north. His reference to this was of a smell of gunpowder. Oliver Stone, too, used a north wind during his reenactment of the assassination. In the Zapruder film, however, we see that the wind came directly out of the south by the woman's blue scarf fluttering in the breeze. Why would a researcher who has studied this film perhaps more than any other individual say the wind was blowing from the north when it wasn't? Did he want someone to prove him wrong? A north wind would have prevented the gunpowder residue from reaching the area of the motorcade where Senator Yarborough and the others noted the odor and where many heard the firecracker noises.

A new book written by Dr. Charles Crenshaw called *Conspiracy of Silence* released this year promotes even more conclusive evidence to the shots striking the president by a frontal attack. In a television interview, Crenshaw, an attending physician who saw the president's wounds, stated that the cerebellum was visible through the back of Kennedy's head. In my opinion Crenshaw, too, is wrong. The Zapruder film and the autopsy photos deny his claim. Why would this doctor who saw the wounds go on national television and say something that could not later be substantiated? These are the efforts which will ultimately bring out the truth. Now ask yourself why?

From the very beginning of my research, I decided that I would not be a part of prefabricating inconsistencies for the purpose of being proven wrong. If as an American I could not tell it like it is, then I wouldn't say anything. Of course once I began researching the event, the more I looked, the more I found. You will see that *Mirror of Doubt* does not contain all the information on the subject relating to President Kennedy's death. If it did, it would take perhaps years to produce and it could not be done alone anyway.

The president has long been reported dead and life must go on.

Though this book documents necessary facts and shares research information and views from others who have reviewed the material here, its main purpose is to produce once again an official inquiry into the death of President Kennedy. Just how conclusive the findings are can only be determined by a grand jury, yet the justice department has since retained the final say in these matters. What does it know that it hasn't told us?

Prior to *Mirror of Doubt* reaching the public, I had intentions of holding onto the information to provide federal law enforcement officials an opportunity to review *Mirror of Doubt*. This would not have prevented the publication of the book, but only preempt it. I did not feel that the American public or perhaps the world should learn about this material prior to the government of the United States making a decision to look into the assassination with a serious interest. It was not the intention of this author to intimidate his government into doing something that it does not feel comfortable with either. Though these were my original intentions, all that has changed.

If the evidence is confusing, then so must the truth be. The truth must be attested to by those who took part in the assassination.

If the facts are clear and the evidence appropriate, people are humans too. I do not want *Mirror of Doubt* to inhibit previously established lines of prosecution or cause an unfair trial for someone other than Lee Harvey Oswald, who did not get a trial. Prior to this writing, I felt if the information contained in *Mirror of Doubt* was to be released prior to a federal investigations, we would have a repeat of Dallas 1963 and perhaps never read the truth. Live and learn. That's also changed.

Chapter Eight

A Final Word

The Kennedy assassination has become an open sore on the integrity of the American government and the burden of proof to change the official ruling has been levied upon only a few hundred individuals. I believe this case was solved on the very afternoon the government reported President John F. Kennedy dead of gunshot wounds from Parkland Hospital, simply because the shooting was too simple not to solve. I believe the confusion of the event turned quickly to subversion and normal governmental procedures to expedite this crime took a back seat to plea bargaining and secrecy. With a creative flip of a pen, the cover-up conspiracy began and a veil of silence was lowered to shield the innocent from shame.

Up until the publishing of *Mirror of Doubt*, only the researchers have had an opportunity to witness the pathetic cause your government used to keep the truth from you. What it did is shameful, without integrity, and plan un-American. It is not what John Kennedy stood for or would have accepted. Because of the mistrust, this decision can not be relished as bearing leadership qualities, faith in God, compassion towards this nation, nor represent justice or the freedoms guaranteed by the Constitution.

Had the assassination been successful, the first shot would have killed the president and Mrs. Kennedy would have died of a second gunshot fired by the assassin. However the plan failed and a second shot could not be risked until the president was dead. By then it was too late. You see in theory, undisclosed by *Mirror of Doubt*, both the president and Mrs. Kennedy were warned that there was a plot to assassinate the president which also included the life of the first lady and there was nothing any head of government could do about it, even if there was a desire.

The president was a very smart man and loved his wife dearly. Since the President was in Dallas at the time this information reached him and plans for the trip had been prearranged months prior to this day, the president found himself at odds which could only be met by staying the course. Dallas provided an unusual but unique setting for an assassination attempt on the president and the assassin used this for an advantage. While nothing could prevent the assassination attempt on Kennedy, the plan's success would rely heavily upon precision and accuracy when shooting and a quick getaway. The uncontrollable would rely on unsubstantiated facts which would become hard boiled by the planted evidence which awaited discovery on the sixth floor of the Depository, there only to confuse a minority of witnesses present in Dealey Plaza during the attempt. Thus the assassin would simply walk away from the crime.

The assassin concentrated on four major elements necessary to successfully killing the president. First, no one was to know when it was going to happen. Therefore the assassin told no one. Orders were sent out to operatives who knew nothing more than an attempt was to be made on the president's life. Many were involved thinking they were there to protect the president, while others served as observers who knew an attempt would occur. No one knew who or how, but everyone knew why.

Second the president of the United States, being the most well-guarded individual in the world, would not be an easy target. Therefore the location from which the shots could be fired was limited to an area in which the president was farthest away from his presidential protection, but would still provide the assassin with an easy getaway and a plausible alibi.

Third, the assassin needed witnesses and thus created a diversion which drew the attention of Secret Service personnel, witnesses in Dealey Plaza, the FBI, CIA operatives, and the president. All eyes were on the president.

Fourth and final, evidence of a gunman and a patsy to unknowingly take the fall. Denial on everyone's part was essential. The risk was high and if the plan was to work, expedience was essential. The fourth element of the assassination was brilliantly executed. While it was necessary to have a patsy take the fall, it was also necessary to develop a strategy sufficient enough to retaining the plan's secrecy. Its implementation was the inspired work of left-wing southerners who deemed it necessary to kill Kennedy, but who also lacked the means and the courage to do so. These people, who were often thought to be as radically boisterous as they were misfits, subsequently played directly into the hands of the assassin.

The left wingers were told of the plot to kill the president and targeted Lee Harvey Oswald as the patsy. Why? Oswald, a CIA operative, had infiltrated the ranks of the left-wing southerners, but his cover was blown while attending a meeting with his superiors. Oswald had to go, so what better way to take care of him. He knew too much and he was inside working for the United States government. When the word trickled down that a pasty was needed, so did the word of Oswald's true identity and cover. Thus Lee Harvey Oswald was set up.

The first phase of the assassination attempt was to make sure that Kennedy and the government in Washington knew of the reported plot beforehand. Once the information reached these people, the FBI and the CIA immediately were called in to investigate the probability of an attempt occurring. Security measures were implemented and the fate of the day remained hopeful. Once the information was let out and word returned to the assassin, that an attempt had been made and security measures were taken, the plan was moved into phase two of the attempt.

The assassin knew that the president would regard the threat and take safety measures of his own, but not to a point where it would infringe upon his flexibility to mingle with his supporters. This was John Kennedy's major weakness and the assassin knew it. Phase two relied heavily on the president to do just what the assassin wanted him to expect the unexpected, but not be ready when the attempt was lodged. As long as the president knew his life was in danger; he would be concerned for the safety of Mrs. Kennedy and would rely on the Secret Service for presidential protection, as he should. The uncertainty of when and where would both satisfy and occupy his curiosity and the advantage would remain the assassin's. At a time when Kennedy least expected danger from an assassin's bullet and relaxed, pulling the actual trigger in an attempt to remove the president from office would be implemented.

It was a well-planned conspiracy and the assassin was as equally motivated by political recognition of the Washington circle and personal satisfaction as was the president. Killing President Kennedy would not be an easy thing to live with, but the respect for such a premeditated act would earn an unconditional pardon from peers, as the identity of the assassin would only be suspected and no charges would ever be filed. The assassin did not hate John Kennedy. If fact President Kennedy had earned much respect and admiration for his perseverance and reverence as a public speaker and domestic policy maker, but Kennedy was in the way of progress and he had to go.

When the shooting began, the assassin once again experienced the pain and guilt which previously engulfed his soul in the months and days preceding 22 November, 1963. The first shot was not intended to be a diversionary one. It was intended to kill the president, but it did not. The plan failed due to human error, but suddenly without warning to the assassin, a second shot was fired from a closely supervised vantage point, striking Governor Connally in the center of his back. While the president struggled to evaluate his own condition and the continued safety for his wife, Jackie, Governor Connally was faced with a near fatal gunshot wound. The suffering became immediately apparent and no choices remained. With two shots fired in less than four seconds, the assassin could no longer perceive the months of planning as being successful. Frustration and anger grew.

The president came to Dallas. Now he must pay. All the assassin could hear was the near silent voice which said, "shoot him again."

The sacrifice was made. Mrs. Kennedy would live but the president must die. From sheer desperation and the fear of reprisal, the assassin in a cold-hearted attempt to renegotiate his failure obeyed the order almost instantaneously and with a second shot fired from the assassin's weapon, history gave way to contempt and the president lay fallen in an atmosphere of despair, frustration, and agony. Mrs. Kennedy, unharmed, cried out in terror, "They shot his head off." Agent Clint Hill guided her back into the blood-soaked limousine and beat his fists angrily on the rear of the car.

As a child I grew up knowing that two wrongs never made a right and that an "eye for an eye" meant more than acting out in vengeance against those who could not or would not accept me for who I am or who I believed in. I also learned, as every researcher has learned, I can convince myself who shot President Kennedy, but should not convince anyone else. Don't get me wrong. I have on many occasions convinced others, but moreover they have convinced me. I have reluctantly conceded to the official version for one simple reason. The assassin must confess to the shooting. It's that simple. Why? For honor. It is the one quality lacking in the life of the assassin. The act of killing a world leader cannot be ordained.

On 22 November, 1963 President Kennedy lay in a hospital recovery room fighting as hard for his life as he did his country. While his children were being comforted the news of the president's fateful trip ripped through the hearts of nearly the entire world. A million bitter tears crept out of the eyes of those who loved Kennedy, while their voices, starving for hope, asked only "Will he survive?"

Governor Connally lay fallen in the hospital room from a bullet which entered his back below the shoulder blade and the president struggled for air to regain the needed oxygen which would supply his life's blood with hope, while surgeons struggled desperately to control the bleeding and loss of cerebral fluid from his head wound. Those who were administering the lifesaving treatment to both men reasoned only in their minds the utter nonsense that brought the men to Parkland Hospital with the mass confusion and eventually would turn the clock of history into a maze of obscurity. There was nothing more said. Only silent thoughts focused on what terrible hope this society thrives on in order to survive.

One can preserve trust, while another a clear conscience. But without honor you are nothing and you have nothing. And so is your part in the fruits of labor. The cost is greater than anyone can imagine.

With regret for all who have suffered; I wish you the best luck when you look into the mirror of doubt. It's sad in a way, what happens to people like myself who have unwittingly walked into the Kennedy case with an open mind, eager only to resolve personal doubt fostered by the confusion of facts which can mean only one thing. I have published *Mirror of Doubt–Can You Solve the JFK Conspiracy?* for one reason and one reason alone. Simply so you do not have to bear the pain that I have researching this case. Just as you look in any mirror, you can see things, describe things, but you cannot reach out and touch them until you have turned around. What makes the future is the present, but the present must first become the past before it becomes our future. What you see in *Mirror of Doubt* is behind you. Make it part of your past.